D0838088

Praise for

Making a Difference

"*Making a Difference* is the first-ever comprehensive review of the RA role from a Christian lens. The authors' ability to frame the extensive components of this time-honored student leadership position using wisdom, formation, and faith development as key paradigms for leadership demonstrates the depth of the RA role. The book length is perfect for student leaders and the short chapters accompanied by discussion questions allow an instructor to easily guide students through this text. With over 100,000 resident assistants in the United States, this ground-breaking book should be an excellent resource for housing departments."

    —**Jeff Doyle**, Dean for Student Learning & Engagement, Baylor University

"A hiker who sets out on a trail knows the value of a good hiking guide that establishes location and direction, describes hazards and challenges along the way, and identifies points of focus so the hiker doesn't miss remarkable vistas. This volume is that kind of resource for the new resident assistant.

    The opening chapters clearly position the role of the resident assistant within the context of higher education, the institution, and the developmental journeys of students. Clear narratives guide the resident assistant through challenging stretches of the journey towards embracing diversity and building community. *Making a Difference* is written with the Christian perspective squarely in focus, which is extraordinarily valuable for those in faith-based institutions. By being attentive to advice provided, a new resident assistant will undoubtedly traverse the ups and downs of the year with sure footing and clarity of purpose. This guide is highly recommended for the resident assistant at Christian Colleges and Universities and those who lead them."

    —**Edee Schulze**, Vice President for Student Life and Dean of Students, Westmont College

"Without a doubt, the resident assistant position provides one of the signature leadership experiences that universities have to offer. This well-written and engaging book covers all the major components of this important role, and does so within a distinctly Christ-centered framework and mission. A book like this is long overdue and will inform and shape Resident Assistant leadership training at Christian institutions for years to come."

    —**Brad Lau**, Vice President for Student Life, George Fox University

"This text is as powerful a resource as there is in equipping your resident assistants to be catalysts for growth and positive transformation within the lives of individual students and your campus community."
—**Paul Blezien**, Vice President for Student Development, Crown College

MAKING A DIFFERENCE

MAKING A DIFFERENCE

Empowering the Resident Assistant

Stephen Beers and Skip Trudeau, editors

Abilene Christian University Press

MAKING A DIFFERENCE
Empowering the Resident Assistant

ACU
PRESS

Copyright 2015 by Stephen T. Beers and C. Skip Trudeau

ISBN 978-0-89112-479-5

Printed in the United States of America

ALL RIGHTS RESERVED
No part of this publication may be reproduced, stored in a retrieval system, or transmitted in any form by any means—electronic, mechanical, photocopying, recording or otherwise—without prior written consent.

Scripture quotations, unless otherwise noted are taken from The Holy Bible, New International Version®, NIV®. Copyright © 1973, 1978, 1984, 2011 by Biblica, Inc.® Used by permission. All rights reserved worldwide.

Scripture quotations noted ESV are from The ESV® Bible (The Holy Bible, English Standard Version®) copyright © 2001 by Crossway, a publishing ministry of Good News Publishers. ESV® Text Edition: 2011. The ESV® text has been reproduced in cooperation with and by permission of Good News Publishers. Unauthorized reproduction of this publication is prohibited. All rights reserved.

Scripture quotations noted *The Message* taken from *The Message.* Copyright 1993, 1994, 1995, 1996, 2000, 2001, 2002. Used by permission of NavPress Publishing Group.

Cover design by Rick Gibson
Interior text design by Sandy Armstrong, Strong Design

Abilene Christian University Press
ACU Box 29138
Abilene, Texas 79699

1-877-816-4455 toll free
www.acupressbooks.com

15 16 17 18 19 20 / 7 6 5 4 3 2 1

Contents

Acknowledgments

We begin by saying a big thank you to the authors of this text who have sacrificed to make this work a reality. A book like this one is born out of reflection on past failures and successes with a deep desire to prepare student leaders to facilitate and flourish in the leadership roles they are called into within the residential community. The residence hall is a powerful place for healing and growth, and the authors of this text have proven to be powerful leaders in the field of student development.

We also acknowledge that our various institutions have made it possible for this text to emerge. The authors have shared the support that has been provided to them by their institution while writing the chapters specifically, Calvin College, John Brown University, Messiah College, Taylor University, Union University, and Wheaton College. This type of relevant writing and research, generated by practitioners in the field, is always aided by institutional support.

The team from Abilene Christian University Press has done a wonderful job assisting in organizing and supporting this edited work. In particular, Leonard Allen has being abundantly gracious about deadlines as we worked around various real life challenges.

And most importantly, we celebrate that our Lord Jesus Christ who is the incarnational savior. He came and dwelt among us. We celebrate our unique callings and the invitation into community.

Sincerely the editors,
Steve Beers & Skip Trudeau

Contributors

Jeff Aupperle (MA, Taylor University) is the Director of the Promising Ventures Program within the Calling and Career Office at Taylor University. He recently graduated from the Master of Arts in Higher Education program at Taylor in which he researched national data from HERI in exploring the role of involvement in students' pursuit of calling. Prior to his graduate studies, Jeff worked in church mobilization with Adventures in Missions (Gainesville, Georgia) and served as a pastor in Romeo, Michigan. Jeff and his family live in Upland, Indiana.

Stephen Beers (EdD, Ball State University) has finished his seventeenth year as Vice President for Student Development at John Brown University. Previously he served at Taylor University and Northwestern College (Iowa). Steve has served as the President of the Association of Christians in Student Development and is currently serving as a Commission Member of the Council for Christian Colleges and Universities. Steve continues to write and speak on issues pertaining to Christian higher education. Previous publications include contributing to and editing *The Soul of the Christian University*, and contributing to and coediting *Funding the Future*. Steve and his wife Jane (Associate Professor of Biology) reside in Siloam Springs, Arkansas.

André Broquard (EdD, University of Arkansas) serves as Dean of Students at John Brown University. He works with Campus Safety, Residence Life, Student Activities, Student Orientation, and Counseling Services. He is active in the Association for Christians in Student Development and currently serves ACSD as Business Chair. André lives with his wife Kristine and four children in Siloam Springs, Arkansas.

Kristin Hansen-Kieffer (EdD, University of South Dakota) is the Vice Provost/Dean of Students at Messiah College. Hansen-Kieffer is also an assistant professor of Exercise Science and has previously held the position of Director of Academic Advising. She has coached volleyball and worked as a Resident Director at other institutions. Hansen-Kieffer has chaired the Master's in Higher Education committee at Messiah College and has also consulted and presented on assessment. She led her team in hosting the ACSD conference at Messiah College in 2010 and currently serves as the organization's president. Her research and publications focus on assessment, wellness, and healthy body image for women. Hansen-Kieffer resides in Dillsburg, Pennsylvania, with her husband and two children.

Sara J. Hightower (MA, Taylor University) is originally from a small town in Ohio. She came to Taylor University as an undergraduate and completed her degree in Christian Educational Ministries. With an interest in ministry and college students, she pursued a Master's in Higher Education and Student Development at Taylor as well. Upon completion of that degree, she served as a Resident Director at Grace College, and returned to Taylor to serve as the Olson Hall Director. She currently works with Residence Life and the Discipleship Program at Taylor as the Director of Residence Life Programs.

Shirley Hoogstra (JD, University of Connecticut School of Law) is Vice President of Student Life at Calvin College, joining Calvin after a career in law, having served as president of the New Haven County Bar Association and chairs of numerous nonprofit, school, and church boards. At Calvin College, she has served on the president's cabinet since July of 1999 and oversees a staff of over ninety professionals, and she originated the Sexuality Series yearly programming, which teaches on topics of human sexuality and faith. She has served in volunteer leadership positions such as leadership development, student development, and intercultural competencies with the Council for Christian Colleges and Universities. She contributed a chapter to *Thriving in Leadership: Strategies for Making a Difference in Christian Higher Education* (ACU Press), edited by Dr. Karen Longman. As cohost of the long-running

PBS program *Inner Compass*, she interviewed many national and international leaders on the topics of faith and human sexuality, diversity, and relationships. Shirley and her family live in Grand Rapids, Michigan, and attend the Mayfair Christian Reformed Church.

Steve Ivester (PhD, Talbot School of Theology) is Dean for Student Engagement at Wheaton College and has been a student-development educator for twenty-one years. He serves as the Scholarship Chair for the Association of Christians in Student Development. His research is directed toward discovering the impact that leadership of social change has on identity development in student activists. Steve mentors many students, encouraging positive attitudes of learning that come through relationship, leadership, and service.

Steve Morley (PhD in progress, Indiana State) is the Dean of Residence Life and Discipleship at Taylor University. He has served in the field of student development for fourteen years—seven years, in a live-in residence-life faculty role and seven years in leadership over the residence-life program at Taylor. Steve and his family live in Upland, Indiana.

Kimberly Thornbury (PhD, Regent University) is the Vice President for Institutional Research and Strategic Planning at The King's College. Previous to her recent move to New York City, Kimberly served as Senior Vice President for Student Services and Dean of Students for fifteen years at Union University in Jackson, Tennessee. She currently serves as chair for Professional Development for the Association of Christians in Student Development. In addition to writing numerous reviews on books related to Christian higher education, Kimberly has written chapters in books including *Faith and Learning: A Handbook for Christian Higher Education* and *Christian Leadership Essentials: A Handbook for Managing Christian Organizations*. Kimberly's husband, Gregory Thornbury, is the president of The King's College, and they live in Manhattan with their two daughters.

C. Skip Trudeau (EdD, Indiana University) is the Vice President for Student Development/Dean of Students at Taylor University. He has served in a number of roles in student development and is a former president of the Association for Christians in Student Development (ACSD). He coauthored *A Parent's Guide to the Christian College: Supporting Your Child's Heart, Soul, and Mind during the College Years* (with Todd C. Ream and Timothy W. Herrmann). He serves as the coeditor (with Timothy W. Herrmann) for *Growth: The Journal of the Association for Christians in Student Development*. Skip and his family live in Upland, Indiana, where they are members of Upland Community Church.

Amy Van Der Werf (EdD in progress, Azusa University) is the Dean of Student Engagement at the University of Northwestern in St. Paul, Minnesota. Amy has worked in higher education for almost twenty years including serving as the Director of Residence Life at Messiah College for eight years. She has also been an active participant in the Association for Christians in Student Development as a member of the Diversity Leadership Team, a leader of the new professionals retreat, and numerous conference presentations. Amy lives in her home state of Minnesota where she appreciates all the seasons but summer most of all.

John Witte (MA, Bowling Green State University) serves as Dean of Residence Life at Calvin College. John began his work at Calvin in 1993 as a resident director. He has served as Assistant Dean and Associate Dean of Residence Life during his tenure, and has been involved in over twenty years of training resident assistants for their work. In addition to the myriad of housing, staffing, and programming aspects of his job, John has served on numerous committees, on topics such as the core curriculum, student retention, and first-year programs. He also oversees a summer leadership program for Calvin students at Snow Mountain Ranch, Granby, Colorado. He and his family live in Grand Rapids, Michigan, and attend First Christian Reformed Church, where John participates as a worship planner and leader.

Doug Wood (MS, Alfred State University) is the Associate Dean of Students at Messiah College, where he has served for over seventeen years in a variety of roles within the Student Affairs Division. Doug started his career at Houghton College, serving as an admissions counselor for his alma mater. Doug is a trained restorative-justice facilitator. His other professional interests include residence-life, student leadership programs, redemptive approaches to student conduct, and making excellence inclusive. Doug also lives in Dillsburg, Pennsylvania, where he serves on the board of the local youth soccer program. Doug and his wife are the parents of two active daughters who love to fish and kayak along the Yellow Breeches Creek.

CHAPTER 1

Introduction

The Calling

SKIP TRUDEAU

The year was 1982 and it was early in the spring semester of my freshman year in college. I was standing outside my residence hall director's (RD) office door, holding in my hand the note he had left in my mailbox (this was in the days before emails and texts) requesting I stop by and see him sometime. I remember feeling a little apprehensive; I wasn't sure if I had done anything to warrant being summoned to see the RD. Nonetheless I knocked on his door and the ensuing conversation went something like this:

> Resident Hall Director: "Come in. Oh hey, it's you. I'm glad you got my note and came to see me. I assume this is a good time."
>
> Me: "Oh sure, can you tell me what this is about? Did I do something wrong?"
>
> Resident Director: (Laughing) "No, in fact I wanted to talk to you about a leadership opportunity that I think you might be good at!"
>
> Me: "Really? What is it?"
>
> Resident Director: "Well, your current RA [resident assistant] and I think you might make a good RA, and I wanted to know if you were interested in applying for next year."

And thus began my nearly-thirty year association with residence-life and resident assistants.

Chances are, if you are reading this book, you also have had a similar conversation with someone who encouraged you to consider becoming an RA, and you have decided that you would pursue this opportunity. This person recognized in you personal qualities such as the desire and willingness to serve, the ability to relate to a wide variety of persons, general leadership skills, and above all the desire to work in a discipleship-focused environment to help others grow. Most likely you have successfully navigated an application and interview process and have been selected to serve as an RA for the upcoming academic year and currently are engaged in a training process or class designed to equip you for the role. If you are anything like I was, you probably have some idea of what an RA does but, you really aren't sure what you have signed on for. That is where this book comes in; it is designed to introduce you to the philosophy and practices associated with residence-life and provide you with tools and insights that will help you as you serve the residents on your floor.

So here you are starting your own RA journey. The year ahead will be many things: exhilarating as you help residents work through a variety of developmental experiences, challenging as you will be placed in the position to apply conduct codes with students on your floor, gut-wrenching as you walk beside residents who have experienced significant trauma, and stretching as you yourself go through a significant amount growth and learning. Being an RA is a very rewarding experience; while you may not be starting a thirty-year career, this experience will shape you for thirty plus years in whatever endeavor your career path leads. The skills you develop here will serve you in whatever path you follow.

This first chapter provides a brief historical sketch of American higher education and the role residence-life has played in this nearly four-hundred-year history. This will be followed by a discussion of the philosophy of residence-life, particularly within the framework of the Christian college setting, and a discussion of the vital role RAs play in this context. Subsequent chapters will deal with student development theory and practice; the spiritual formation of college students; the role of the RA in developing and maintaining campus culture and intentional community; developmental programming; confrontation and institutional discipline; RA self-care; peer counseling; and leading/interacting with diverse populations. This book is designed to help prepare RAs for service in the Christian college.

Residence Life History

Two major characteristics of the earliest colleges founded in this country are particularly germane to this discussion. First and foremost, the earliest institutions of higher learning in this country were Christian in nature. Second, they were almost exclusively residential in nature.

Beginning with the founding of Harvard College in 1636 by Puritan Congregationalists,[1] Protestant denominational leaders were the single leading force in starting and developing higher education in the new world. All but one of the nine colleges founded in the colonies prior to the start of the Revolutionary War were birthed by specific denominational initiatives aimed at promoting the doctrinal interpretation and lifestyle expectations associated with that denomination. That one school, The College of Philadelphia, soon came to be under the influence of the Anglican Church. The nine colonial colleges and their founding denominations are shown in Table 1.

Table 1: Colonial Colleges and Founding Denominations[2]	
Harvard 1636	Congregationalists
William and Mary 1693	Anglican
Yale 1701	Congregationalists
Princeton 1746	Presbyterian
Kings* 1754	Anglican
Pennsylvania 1755	Secular-Anglican
Brown 1765	Baptists
Queens** 1766	Dutch Reformed
Dartmouth 1769	Congregationalists

* Kings was renamed Columbia after the Revolutionary War

** Queens was renamed Rutgers after the Revolutionary War

This clearly demonstrates that the founding of higher education in America was inextricably connected to Protestant denominations and that these earliest colleges were founded to pursue Christian purposes, along with civic and vocational ends.

We can conclude that Christian institutions have always been a part of the landscape of American higher education. Not only this, but in the prerevolutionary-war period, Christian higher education was the only form available to those wishing to pursue education beyond what would have been considered at the time secondary or even primary education. Today modern Christian colleges do not play as dominant or primary a role; if one looks at the current makeup of higher education, these institutions can appear to be a small and somewhat insignificant presence in a field that seems dominated by larger public institutions. This has occurred through a process called secularization[3] which refers to a process in which a college or university moves from a primarily religious focus in all programs to one that downplays or minimizes the role of religion. It eventually results in a systematic de-emphasis of any religious orientation. For example, none of the nine colleges founded prior to the Revolutionary War would now consider themselves to have anything more than a historical connection to Protestantism even though they began with a clearly identified sense of being what modern scholars would call Christian colleges. This secularization process has resulted in the Christian college moving from a central place in higher education to a role of much reduced influence as measured by the number of institutions still pursuing a primarily Christian agenda and the number of students enrolled in these schools.

The second important historical element is the fact that a form of residence-life has also always been present in American higher education. From the earliest colonial colleges, in a time when students left their homes and lived together at the college, until today, when residential programs are still very prominent in American colleges and universities, living on and/or near the college is a hallmark of our higher educational system.

For the earliest schools, practicality was the primary driver for students living on site. These schools had small enrollments and correspondingly small faculty—often one to three professors, including a president—so all students and staff lived together. As enrollments and staff grew, so did the need for additional housing options. Many schools opted to build residence halls, then called dormitories, as a means to house and help monitor students. Remember that these early schools were interested in the piety of their students as well as their academic progress. Campus "dorms" became more and more prominent, and it is only within the last hundred years that community colleges, online programs, and for-profit educational programs have come into being, providing virtually no on-campus living accommodations for students. It is still safe to say, however, that residential living is a hallmark of the American system and is a distinguishing characteristic for a majority of colleges and universities.

There were no student development professionals in the earliest American colleges. The out-of-classroom activities of students were monitored by those who taught in the classrooms. This was true until the late 1800s when the first professional student development administrators began finding their way onto campuses. This was largely due to increased specialization on the part of professors and increased enrollments. The first student resident assistants started appearing after the turn of the twentieth century, and the RA has emerged as a prominent fixture in residential programs. These paraprofessional staff persons have become a vital component of the coeducational programing on the majority of American college and university campuses.

Why is this history important to this discussion? There are at least two reasons. First, it speaks to the primary focus of this book: to prepare RAs for service in Christian colleges. Residential programing on Christian college campuses has not received much attention in higher education literature. One of the main goals of this book is to fill that void and provide a practical guide to those engaging in this endeavor. Second, it is encouraging and even inspiring to know that the roles in which we serve have such a distinguished heritage.

Philosophy of Residence Life

One unique feature of higher education in the United States is the existence of a strong cocurricular program, most often in the form of athletics and programs such as residence-life, student activities, orientation, student government organizations, special interest clubs and organizations, and others. This system has been referred to as a "bifurcated"[4] because historically the two sides—academic and student development—have functioned somewhat separately from each other. In the best-case scenarios the relationship between the two was amicable. In less than desirable situations the two have been at odds, and at times actual animosity has existed on some campuses as the two sides grappled for resources and status. This tension has abated somewhat in more recent times due to the growing sense that both the academic and student development programs are valuable and contribute to the overall development of college students. Instead of working against each other, the two sides have become much more tolerant of each other on most campuses. This amicable relationship is especially true for the majority of Christian college campuses, where the development of a student's faith and intellect forms the core outcome. Indeed Christian higher education tends to view the two as inseparable.[5]

Arguably one of the most important scholarly contributions to Christian higher education was the publication of *The Idea of the Christian College* by Arthur Holmes.[6] In this seminal work, Holmes developed a concept that has become the mantra for Christian higher education: "the integration of faith and learning." The basic premise of the integration of faith and learning is that the cognitive development that occurs in the college experience is compatible with spiritual development and that the two can and should be fostered simultaneously in a nurturing environment. This philosophy is prevalent at institutions that identify themselves as Christian colleges and is the subject of much discussion both on these campuses and at professional meetings. This philosophical stand is what distinguishes Christian higher education from the rest of American higher education. It is important to remember that currently Christian colleges are not viewed by other sectors of higher education as significant players, so the integration of faith and learning has become a rallying point and anchor for Christian institutions.

Whole-person education is another important concept in the Christian college context and fits nicely with the integration of faith and learning. The basic premise is that during the college experience students develop across multiple domains—intellectual, spiritual, emotional, vocational, and physical—therefore the educational program should be structured to foster development in these multiple dimensions. In other words, the collegiate experience, while focused on the intellectual domain, should also intentionally foster growth in these other areas as well: it should develop the whole person.

For those working in the student-development or student-affairs field, this approach has developed into a cornerstone of our practice and provides much needed structure and guidance to our efforts. This is particularly true for those who practice within the Christian college context; we have the added dimension of spiritual growth to design our programs around. This whole-person approach forms the foundation for the development of organized co-curricular (or out-of-class) programs that work in concert with curricular (in classroom) programs. We, the authors of this book, believe that this is the most ideal context for learning to occur.

Intentional community is a third important concept for the philosophical discussion of the role of the RA in Christian colleges. Intentional community in this context refers to the systematic and purposeful approach in which student development programs are designed and implemented to foster student growth in their intellectual, spiritual, emotional, physical, and vocational development. This sense of intentionality allows student development staff to offer programs that bridge the gap between classroom learning and the learning that takes place in less formal settings such as residence hall and others. Intentionality implies a systematic approach in which co-curricular programs are meticulously designed and carefully implemented to achieve the learning and developmental goals of the program. The goal is that in both of these settings—formal classroom and out-of-class—students' experiences will enhance each other, thus creating an intentionally holistic environment in which the integration of faith and learning can flourish. This mutually beneficial relationship has been referred to as a "seamless learning environment"[7] in which all student experiences enhance learning and growth.

Philosophically, the integration of faith and learning, whole person education, intentional community, and seamless learning environments form the conceptual framework for the majority of student development practitioners at Christian colleges. But what role does the resident assistant play? Simply put, the RA is one of the most important players in this process. Each year I have the privilege of addressing incoming RAs as they assume their positions. I always start by saying "We [referring to the university where we serve] win or lose the battle for community at the RA level." While you might think I am guilty of overstating my position, I firmly believe this is true. RAs by virtue of living in residence halls serve a critically vital role. They, along with professional live-in staff, the residence hall directors, are the front line for accomplishing the goals of faith-learning integration, whole person education, and intentional community. As I state every year to our RAs, we would not be successful without their efforts. RAs serve as liaison between professional staff and residents as well as provide a real-time model for other students. Simply put, if RAs live out the goals we have been talking about, then there is a much higher likelihood that those around them will as well. Without dedicated RAs, the tasks of faith-learning integration, whole-person education, and intentional community are much more difficult to achieve.

This may sound like a great deal of pressure to put on RAs; after all; you are students too, and while you are diligently seeking all of these aspects for your residents, you too are still working through many of the same developmental challenges. Rest assured that the professional staff who selected you will also be very intentional in training and supporting you through this process. Reading this book indicates that the professional student development staff at your college is serious about preparing you for the year ahead and that they will be there to support you through the challenges you will face. Nearly every residence-life program I am aware of puts RA candidates through a fairly rigorous application process followed by an equally thorough training program. And when you're on the job, resident directors and other professional staff will provide ongoing support and training.

Conclusion

In this introductory chapter we have briefly discussed the history of residence-life and the role of faith in the context of American higher education. From the beginning both have been part of the American college landscape. Next came a discussion of current philosophy of Christian higher education residence-life programs and the vital role resident assistants play in achieving the goals of faith-learning integration, whole-person education, and intentional community. It is our prayer for you as you begin this journey as a resident assistant that you will be successful in your tasks and that you will grow spiritually and intellectually as you help those around you do the same. It is our hope that this book will prove to be useful in helping you prepare for this significant responsibility.

DISCUSSION QUESTIONS

Take a few moments and answer the questions. Jot down some of your thoughts under the questions for further discussion with the staff.

1. How would you describe the commitment of your institution to the integration of faith and learning, whole-person education, and intentional community?

2. What role does the residence-life program on your campus play in working towards these goals?

3. What would a "seamless learning environment" look like on your campus? In your living unit?

4. How will you as a resident assistant foster the intellectual, spiritual, and emotional growth and health of the residents in your living unit?

ACTIVITIES

1. Make a list of educational and social programs you can imagine implementing in your living unit that will help you foster this growth.

2. Develop a list of persons on your campus who you think understand the integration of faith and learning at your institution and make an appointment with two to three of them, asking them to describe how they see this integration happening on your campus.

3. Read a copy of your institution's history (every campus has one or more) and trace how faith-learning integration has occurred.

CHAPTER 2

The Role of the Resident Assistant in Fulfilling a University's Mission

Being Part of a Larger Purpose

Stephen Beers

Have you ever thought seriously about the meaning of the word "mission" in the context of a company, an organization, or an institution? It is a concise statement that outlines the organization's purpose and provides a path that guides its decision-making. Once a mission is formulated, the statement then directs and drives the actions of each member of the organization. For example, the Chick-Fil-A restaurant chain's mission statement, "*To be American's best quick-service restaurant*," reveals their commitment to service.

Academic institutions also have mission statements that are often based on the answers to questions such as: What characteristics will be instilled in the graduates of our institution? What values will they model to society? What impact will they make in the world? Every academic institution is driven by its own particular mission and spends significant time and resources to fulfill these objectives. Although most campus community members grasp the primary aspects of its mission, it is a complex task for them to gain a comprehensive understanding of the mission and to identify their own particular roles in fulfilling it.

On a college campus, fulfilling the mission is often complicated due to the varying and diverse roles of faculty, staff, and administrators. For this reason, it is even more important for all members of the campus community, including its student leaders, to share common goals that are mission-driven. Resident assistants are members of the student development staff and they are both a legitimate and an important member of the university's leadership team. Thus, the mission of your institution should direct and shape the way you accomplish your responsibilities.

You play an important role in fulfilling the university's mission by shaping your residential community's culture. You do this by using real-life experiences to teach life lessons, and by leveraging unique, real-time moments that enable holistic development among your fellow students. Before we delve deeper into this topic, it might be helpful for you to take a moment to find and reflect on the mission statement of your institution.

Understanding Your Role

In order to help you better understand your role as an RA in fulfilling the mission of your college, let's look at the following institutional mission statement:

> *"John Brown University provides Christ-centered education that prepares people to honor God and serve others by developing their intellectual, spiritual, and professional lives."*[1]

In a cursory review, the RAs at JBU might not immediately identify either themselves or their daily responsibilities as being impacted by this mission statement. But upon deeper reflection, it becomes apparent that virtually all their endeavors are drawn from its developmental focus. For example, central to providing a *"Christ-centered education"* is the concept of the incarnation— the presence of Christ in this world. As followers of Jesus Christ, the RA models this incarnational aspect of the mission by recognizing that his or her role is to become the hands and feet of Christ within the campus community.

Going a bit further into this mission statement, most Christian educators would agree that you cannot fully prepare students *"to honor God and serve others"*[2] outside of a communal context—a place where real life is practiced and real learning is embraced. Resident assistants serve in a 24/7, integrated position that is embedded inside the campus community. Their decisions and actions have the potential to make a substantial impact on the culture of a campus. As a consequence, the work of the RA is paramount to the fulfillment of the mission, and residence-life staff play a central role in the holistic development of the students who attend the university.

The RAs are key representatives and leaders of the institution. The manner in which they carry out their responsibilities both exposes and defines the priorities of the campus community. The RAs' appropriate management of acceptable behaviors and attitudes of residents enhance their students' ability to effectively interact with and be influenced by the faculty, staff, and administration. Carrying out these responsibilities leads to the fulfillment of the remaining portion of the mission by "*developing [students'] intellectual, spiritual, and professional lives.*"[3]

Let's further explore five aspects of an RA's responsibilities that directly impact a campus community and thus play a key role in fulfilling the mission.

1. *You shape culture.* In his text *Culture Making: Recovering our Creative Callings* (2008), Andy Crouch outlines the Christian believer's responsibility to shape and create culture. Crouch's work is written to motivate and direct all Christians to engage the world and shape the larger culture, but his words have particular significance to student leaders who lead and support their residential communities. This is illustrated by a few prominent quotes: "Of all the things cultures conserve most carefully—of all that they are most committed to cultivate—among the most important are ritual and time."[4] At first, you might think that you have no rituals in your hall, but in fact you do. A ritual could be something as simple as when your hall "settles down at night" or the stories that are told about the students who lived there in the past. The cultural components of your hall shape your residents' understanding of what it means to be a part of your living area—and eventually a member of your college community. More than any other group at a residential college, RAs shape the institution's culture, which in turn enables the college to fulfill its mission. The lesson here is that you directly impact the culture of your living community through the rituals you establish, shape, and/or support.

In addition, you influence your residents by helping them choose where and how they spend their time.

Crouch also states, "All culture making is local . . . culture always starts small."[5] It is important for you to recognize that you are a leader, and by simply starting with small cultural changes, you can work to reshape cultural norms. It is worthwhile to spend some time as a "cultural anthropologist," uncovering the artifacts from your residential community and deciphering the messages your particular community is intentionally or unintentionally communicating. Most likely your residents will be able to easily tell you the characteristics that define or are valued by the men and/or women in your living area. Your efforts will establish cultural artifacts that result in positive change to your current residential culture and will impact those living in it for the rest of their lives. Shaping culture also happens as you respond to situations that arise and as you speak for the institution. We will have more on these culture-shaping activities later in this chapter.

2. *You educate through experiences*. Educational theorists have researched and written extensively about how people learn and change. In the early 1900s, John Dewey challenged the teaching methods of the academic institutions of his day and went on to establish a different understanding of learning processes. His new idea prominently included the element of experience. In *Experience and Education* Dewey wrote, "There is one permanent frame of reference: namely, the organic connection between education and personal experience."[6] He noted later in the book that "education in order to accomplish its ends both for the individual learner and for society must be based upon experience."[7] Both experiential educators and student-development theorists have since converged on this notion that when educators harness and facilitate "experience," it becomes a powerful tool for learning.

Furthermore, higher education is currently going through significant reform. University leaders are being challenged to move beyond defining education as a simple acquisition of knowledge and are instead being called to include "critical competencies" in the university's curriculum. These experiential competencies include such attributes as developing interpersonal and team skills, critical thinking, developing respect for others and self, along with the ability to take personal responsibility and to act ethically.[8] It is interesting to note that all of these competencies directly align with the learning goals and objectives of most residence-life programs. These leading educational thinkers continue to push open the door for the inclusion of the residential-program's goals as a significant component of the fulfillment of the institution's mission. You as an RA are an experiential educator.

3. *You educate in real-time within the community.* As more fully developed in other chapters in this text, the holistic development of students is facilitated in a large part by the day-to-day interaction within the campus-wide community. Student-development theory outlines the significant changes that await the college student, which can be powerfully facilitated by the ongoing experiences that take place within the residence halls. Whether it is developing autonomy from one's family or establishing competencies in specific life skills, the daily responsibilities of RAs are essential in challenging and supporting these incremental changes in their residents. It is also important for you to recognize that a "teachable moment," the time when individuals are most ready to learn and change, can come at any time. The catalyst for such a change of thinking or habit cannot always be defined ahead of time; therefore, the available RA who is part of the living, learning community of residence life has a perfect opportunity to direct and facilitate significant learning experiences.

Pause and think for a moment about the potential that exists for you to significantly impact your residents through your leadership. The remainder of this chapter provides practical wisdom to RAs who see their role as mission-driven.

4. *You are a first responder.* Fulfilling the institutional mission by living and leading from inside the community places the RA in a "first responder" position in many situations. How leaders respond when situations arise shapes an organization's culture and provides opportunity to further the organization's mission. Navigating this particular responsibility is both challenging and complicated, so the following suggestions can provide some assistance.

- *Make an assessment of the situation.* This can be a formal or informal process, but an assessment of the situation needs to be done in order to appropriately organize needed resources and direct an appropriate response. Most situations that an RA will encounter will be discussed in RA training along with expectations of what the RA is to do.

- *Prepare for the mundane and the unique situations.* As stated above, RA training will provide you with direction on appropriate responses to most situations you will face. Responding appropriately will take practice and skill. Some situations virtually every RA will face, such as assisting residents with difficult relationships, stress, or conflict. But other situations that staff prepare for most RAs will thankfully never face, like managing a response to a damaging tornado.

- *In every situation, RAs will need to acknowledge and work within their limitations.* Your limitations are set externally by the role that you play as well as internally by your own personal strengths. Know your limits and work within the system to draw on your strengths and manage your weaknesses. When possible, the best time to organize the resources necessary to respond to a need is not when the need arises. This also means that the RA needs to be ready to both ask for and acquire assistance.

- *You must eventually act.* All preparation and training is developed with the assumption that the RA is going to take action. Some individuals have a more difficult time deciding when to act or when to continue to gather additional and more accurate information on any given issue. For all leaders, the time will come when action is required and postponing a leadership decision will actually hamper your success.

5. *You are a communicator for the university*. Leadership is about action, but it also requires accurate and timely communication. Good information arrests inappropriate fears and guides people in the right direction. Communication shapes individual perceptions and ultimately the culture. The RA has a strategic role in being a liaison between students and the administration. A good liaison knows the wants and needs of each party and wants to communicate effectively back and forth between the two by using language that facilitates understanding. A good liaison translates, when needed, what the other group is attempting to say.

In many situations, an RA is placed in the role of informal spokesperson. A simple illustration of this is the RA's responsibility to communicate to residents about lifestyle expectations or explain why tuition rates have increased. A good spokesperson gives an organization "human form," allowing the audience (your students) the ability to connect on a personal level.[9] A spokesperson uses inclusive language and builds trust and credibility for the institution. If the RA has established a positive and trusted relationship with her residents, and the university administration views her as trustworthy, then she can communicate difficult information in a way that will gain support for an institution or at least better understanding and more accurate information.

Maximizing Your Role

The work that an RA does on campus is challenging yet rewarding. In order to do your job well, you need to know yourself, which includes knowing your strengths and weaknesses. By identifying what you are good at and where you will need assistance, you are more likely not only to lean into your strengths but also to seek assistance for the responsibilities that you are more likely to struggle to accomplish. By acknowledging that you will be good at some things but not great at everything, you can then define and organize your work accordingly. Here are some suggestions to maximize your abilities as an RA:

Stay grounded. Being grounded means not only knowing yourself and understanding how God sees you but also staying intimately connected to him. Although there is not ample room for a full discussion here, scripture paints a magnificent picture of how God sees us in all our human frailty. He is not surprised by your weaknesses and limitations. Embracing a biblical understanding of who you are in Christ will direct your actions and attitudes. Accepting the truths of scripture also frees you from the pitfalls of confusion regarding success and failure. When you choose to stay grounded, you minister from a solid foundation of knowing who you are from God's perspective and what you have been made to do well.

Lead from inside the community. As suggested earlier, the role of RAs is unique in that they carry out their responsibilities while being fully immersed in the community. A parallel example of "leading from within" would be how a player-coach gives steady direction to the team while still fully engaged in the athletic contest. This duality of immersion and leadership can complicate relationships and can even limit the RA's opportunities. Therefore, it is critical that the RA remain as approachable as possible. As with any relationship, each member has some responsibility in the relationship's success or failure, but the RA who can remain approachable and available has a better chance of demonstrating superior leadership from within the community.

Be authentic and humble. Authenticity has always been a hallmark of good leadership, especially within Christian circles. To be truly authentic you need to have a right understanding of who you are in relationship to God and your peers. Real humility starts with a full grasp of your own fallen nature as well as the acknowledgment that all humans reflect God's image and thus have eternal value. Authenticity for Christian believers requires us to live our lives in a transparent manner, not to unload our own burdens and thus walk more lightly alone, but to intentionally share the burdens of others and carry them to the cross that liberated us. Authenticity in the leadership position of an RA invokes a posture of servant leadership, a deep and genuine love for others and true humility. As Tim Keller writes, "The essence of gospel-humility is not thinking more of myself or thinking less of myself, it is thinking of myself less."[10] Clearly this is some practical advice that is definitely worth heeding.

Be available. Another foundational component to being a successful RA is being consistently available to your residents. On the surface this may sound like an easy task, but most individuals will find this to be one of the more difficult aspects of the job. Whether you are an introvert or extrovert, a type A or B personality, or whether you excel or struggle with time management, the commitment to being available and fully present is essential. Balancing one's school work, personal relationships, and extracurricular commitments with the needs (real or perceived) of your residents is a challenge. But the RA who is available to her residents at the appropriate level has a better opportunity to accomplish the various tasks and goals of the residential program. Scripture chronicles God's consistent story of being available and present in concrete ways, with the most spectacular example being the incarnation of Christ and his physical presence with us.

There is an old saying that anyone walking through the woods has a difficult time seeing both the totality of the forest as well as the individual trees. Being present and available provides opportunities for you to see both the "forest" and the "trees." It is a difficult task to see individual and personal situations while also assembling individuals into a whole and then determining how that unit fits into the larger residential program. However, RAs have a unique vantage point. By being fully immersed in their floor, they can see each student as a unique individual, all the while gaining perspective from conversations with other staff who can provide a larger picture of the whole community. This ability "to see the trees and the forest" gives RAs a unique opportunity to gain critical information that provides direction and dissipates misunderstandings.

Getting Prepared

An RA must spend time in preparation. The more prepared you are for the various responsibilities you will encounter, the better chance you will have for success. To that end, most colleges have either an RA and/or a leadership class during which the university faculty and staff teach the RAs about the expectations of the position. This can be a rewarding time that provides you a comprehensive understanding of the rationale behind the specific expectations outlined for the RAs on your campus.

Beyond the specific training that takes place on campus, many RAs have also been in other leadership positions before coming to campus or before being hired as an RA. The lessons you may have already learned in previous roles such as a camp counselor or a team captain can be helpful in maximizing your role as an RA. It is beneficial to connect what you have learned in previous leadership positions to that of being an RA.

The summers during your college years are full of rich opportunities and new experiences along with unexpected trials and tribulations. As you return to campus to take on the responsibilities of being an RA, it is important for you to discuss with your residence-life staff any significant life experiences. These conversations can enable you to take on unique responsibilities within your work as an RA or to request additional support.

Gathering Support

As an RA, it is also essential for you to remember that you are not alone in your work. A wide variety of campus and local community members are both willing and waiting to partner with you in the fulfillment of your responsibilities. The following is a list of those available on most campuses.

Student development staff (SD). The residential life staff are usually part of a larger student development department on your campus. The SD department can include staff members from career development, diversity, health services, activities, leadership development, and orientation, as a few examples. These staff members are all working together to accomplish similar goals. They are also individuals who have been around a little longer and are in regular contact with your resident director. In addition, they usually have student staff members whom you may know or who live on your floor. All of these individuals are looking forward to partnering with you to fulfill their own goals.

Faculty members are central to fulfilling a university's mission. The classroom is usually where you can find most professors, but the role of the faculty member on many campuses is expanding. Many faculty members understand that they can enhance the impact they have on their students by partnering with residence-life staff. It is becoming more of a norm among academicians to view the residence hall as a powerful living and learning lab that can support the educational goals of the classroom. You should take full advantage of partnering with faculty and their expertise and seek ways to provide them with creative opportunities to develop meaningful relationships with your residents.

Administrators and other staff members on your campus have come to work at your institution because of their belief in its mission. Their work can often go unnoticed by students, but they also can be called upon to assist the RA in a variety of programming efforts or direct student support.

The list of people you can partner with does not have to end with the traditional campus community. There are seminary staff, graduate faculty, local pastors, business leaders, international ministry staff members—virtually anyone you can think of who is willing to assist you. You are not alone, and most individuals you think would be able to help are just waiting to be asked.

Conclusion

In conclusion, as an RA you play a crucial role in the fulfillment of your institution's mission. You not only shape campus culture but also facilitate experiential learning. You are part of the campus-wide, first responder-team, and you are responsible to provide accurate and appropriate communication. Yet, it is important for you to remember that your role is somewhat limited as a student-staff person, and you will need to limit your responses to those areas that are within your authority. These boundaries should be seen as a way to protect you and are not intended to restrict you from appropriate ministry. These limitations will actually allow you to sustain and succeed in your multiple roles as an RA. Remember, you are part of a larger staff that is there to support and encourage you in your work, studies, and personal development. The RA has always played a central role in the fulfillment of a university's mission. You now have the opportunity to carry on this tradition.

DISCUSSION QUESTIONS

Take a few moments and answer the questions. Jot down some of your thoughts under the questions for further discussion with the staff.

1. Write or summarize your institution's mission statement. Where do you fit in?

2. List some of your living area's cultural norms.

3. Assess if these norms are helping or hurting your ability to help fulfill the mission.

4. Who are the persons in the administration that you can talk to and whom should you get to know?

5. What will be the difficult aspect of being "available"?

6. What will be the difficult aspect of leading from the "inside"?

7. What are the limits in being "authentic" as a student leader?

Activities

1. Jot down specific activities that you will be doing as an RA that directly relate to fulfilling the institution's mission.

2. Make a list of three cultural norms that you would like to support or establish for your area.

3. Describe a situation where you learned a lesson from living in the residence hall.

4. Make a list of the people who will be your support team.

CHAPTER 3

The Role of the Resident Assistant
in Applying Student Development Theory

How It All Works

Jeff Aupperle and Skip Trudeau

Every episode of the original *Star Trek* television series began with the following monologue by Captain James T. Kirk (played by William Shatner): "Space: the final frontier. These are the voyages of the Starship Enterprise. Its five-year mission: to explore strange new worlds, to seek out new life and new civilizations, to boldly go where no man has gone before." If you have ever watched one of these original episodes, you will find it hard to believe that in its day it was the cutting edge of television and special effects. I want to focus in on the last phrase by Captain Kirk: "to boldly go where no man has gone before" as it sums up how I used to think about engaging in student affairs work. In fact, I once used this exact phrase during a presentation at one of the first professional conferences I ever attended.

The year was 1986 and I had been asked to sit on a panel of new professionals speaking to a group of veteran, student-development practitioners at the annual conference for the Association of Christians in Student Development. I had just completed the first year of a two-year masters program in student development and I was a little over-confident in my burgeoning knowledge about my future profession. The panelists were asked to give our initial impressions after our first year or so of service. I thought I had really prepared well for this assignment and had chosen to use these fateful words of Captain Kirk as a humorous way to introduce my comments about my foray into the uncharted academic territory of student development theory and practice.

What I failed to realize then, and what I think many still often fail to realize today, is that the field of student development is based on a rich theoretical heritage and that it is a legitimate field of academic study. The specific study is limited to graduate work but nonetheless offers a theoretical framework upon which good residential life programs are based.

The purpose of this chapter is to introduce some of the most prominent theories applicable to residence-life which will in turn help you appreciate the importance of the work in which you are engaging.

Foundations of Student-Development Theory

In constructing a theoretical framework for understanding the expansion of student development theory over time, the work of Erik Erikson provides an apt foundation from which to start. Student-affairs administrators "first turned to psychologists (for example Erikson, 1950, 1968; Piaget, 1952) for information about human development that would help them to understand the students with whom they were working."[1]

While Erikson's foundational theory of psychosocial development spanned an entire lifetime, institutions of higher education place their focus on what Astin termed *Four Critical Years*. Accordingly, Erikson's stages five, six, and seven—Identity vs. Role Confusion, Intimacy vs. Isolation, and Generativity vs. Stagnation—are the most salient for student development practitioners. The eight stages offered by Erikson built upon the bedrock of Sigmund Freud's psychosexual stages while emphasizing the development of the ego in lieu of sexual development. Erikson's theory emphasizes the critical nature of activities and factors that promote identity achievement, including: varied roles, decision-making, meaningful achievement, freedom from anxiety, and time for reflection.[2]

The following stages, as delineated by Erikson, pointed to a primary virtue achieved in each of the eight phases of development:

- Trust vs. Mistrust (oral-sensory); *Virtue: Hope*
- Autonomy vs. Shame (muscular-anal); *Virtue: Will*
- Initiative vs. Guilt (locomotor-genital); *Virtue: Purpose*
- Industry vs. Inferiority (latency); *Virtue: Competence*
- Identity vs. Role Confusion (adolescence); *Virtue: Fidelity*
- Intimacy vs. Isolation (young-adulthood); *Virtue: Love*
- Generativity vs. Stagnation (middle adulthood); *Virtue: Care*
- Ego Integrity vs. Despair (late adulthood); *Virtue: Wisdom*[3]

Practically speaking, educators can implement Erikson's theory through programming and activities that encourage the development of students' fidelity and love as they navigate the developmental stages of latency and adolescence. As student development professionals reflect on their own psychosocial development during their college years, it offers unique perspective from which to share with students. Active engagement in reflection and mentoring demonstrates a distinctive emphasis on actualizing the larger purpose of student development, namely, the education and development of the whole person.

Arthur Chickering articulated a similar purpose forty-five years ago: "Building on Erikson's discussion of identity and intimacy, Chickering saw the establishment of identity as the core developmental issue with which students grapple during their college years."[4] Chickering championed the idea that the mandate of the academy is not just education, but *Education and Identity*. Chickering's seven vectors were as follows:

- Developing competence
- Managing emotions
- Moving through autonomy toward interdependence
- Developing mature interpersonal relationships
- Establishing identity
- Developing purpose
- Developing integrity.[5]

Chickering identified these as vital developments in the cultivation of men and women who would be better prepared for meaningful contributions to society.

In comparison with other prominent student-development theories, Chickering's influential vectors are often delineated as being closer to stages. However, these stages are not linear or sequential, and the establishment of identity is the central developmental focus. Chickering places heavy emphasis on environmental influences, including: emotional, interpersonal, ethical, and intellectual elements; students will move through the seven vectors at varying rates and may return to areas previously resolved.[6]

Student development professionals can employ Chickering's theory and associated vectors to help students progress from developing competence to the desired end of developing integrity. Chickering's vectors are useful in creating classroom experiences, programming, and other extra-curricular activities to help students progress in the development of identity.

Cognitive-Structural Theories

Moving to cognitive-structural theories, the work of Swiss developmental psychologist Jean Piaget is essential. Piaget's developmental theory introduced four stages that span the cognitive development of human knowledge:

- Sensorimotor: Birth to 18–24 months
- Preoperational: Toddlerhood (18–24 months) to early childhood (age 7)
- Concrete operational: Ages 7 to 12
- Formal operational: Adolescence through adulthood[7]

Piaget's theory of cognitive development laid the groundwork for future cognitive developmental theory and served as the forerunner to the work of other theorists such as Perry, Kohlberg, Gilligan, and Kolb.[8]

William Perry built on Piaget's work, focusing on how students make meaning. Perry's theory focuses on the move from categorical or dualistic thinking toward more complex understandings. The process Perry proposes moves from dualism to multiplicity to contextual relativism, concluding in commitment.

Perry's theory includes nine positions of development that one moves through toward the achievement of intellectual and ethical development:

- Position 1: Basic Duality
- Position 2: Dualism: Multiplicity Pre-legitimate
- Position 3: Multiplicity Subordinate or Early Multiplicity
- Position 4: Complex Dualism and Advanced Multiplicity
- Position 5: Relativism
- Position 6: Relativism: Commitment Foreseen
- Positions 7 through 9: Levels of Commitment[9]

Student development educators can implement Perry's theory in their work to help students move from a dualistic way of thinking toward the development of commitment. Students often enter college with a markedly black and white view of the world. The formative years of college bring students into encounters with a more complex way of thinking. Students must navigate the transition from dualism and the challenges of relativism in moving toward achieving enduring commitment. Relationship development in the residence halls and varying experiences in cocurricular activities can help students move through the positions presented by Perry.

Moral Development Theories

The developmental theory introduced by Erikson and Piaget offered a firm base on which to create refined understandings of moral development. Consequently, building on Erikson and Piaget's foundation, Lawrence Kohlberg and Carol Gilligan constructed theories that can be of practical use in the moral development of college students.

Kohlberg posits that morality is achieved through socialization and internalization of cultural/family norms; moral development varies, however, based on cultural and gender differences. Kohlberg's theory describes a progression of moral development from an external, rule-oriented sense of morality to an internal, principle-oriented sense of morality.[10]

Kohlberg's theory has three levels with two stages of development within each level:

- Level 1: Pre-conventional Morality
    - Stage 1: Heteronomous
    - Stage 2: Individualism, instrumental purpose and exchange
- Level 2: Conventional Morality
    - Stage 3: Mutual interpersonal expectations, relationships, and interpersonal conformity
    - Stage 4: Social systems morality
- Level 3: Post-conventional Morality
    - Stage 5: Social contract or utility and individual rights
    - Stage 6: Universal ethical principles[11]

Kohlberg's theory is applicable in helping students to reason morally. Such development can be achieved in residence halls through resolving moral dilemmas and interpersonal problems. In addition, moral development is often fostered through community service/service learning opportunities and interaction with faculty outside of the classroom.

The development of moral reasoning in students is beneficial for the entire campus as students will learn to make better decisions both academically and socially. Educators should consider the variances that exist based on an individual upbringing, students' understanding of cultural and family norms, and how gender differences affect the rate of development.

In light of the emphasis on gender differences, Carol Gilligan focused on care as opposed to the justice orientation of Kohlberg. Gilligan suggests that the development of moral reasoning is vastly different in women—who Gilligan believed were underrepresented in Kohlberg's theory. According to Gilligan, women reason and speak very differently when challenged by a moral dilemma.[12] Gilligan emphasized non-violence, understanding and valuing the needs of others, and interconnectedness. Gilligan's theory has three stages and two transitions:

- Pre-conventional—Goal is individual survival
- *Transition*—Selfishness to responsibility to others
- Conventional—Self-sacrifice is goodness
- *Transition*—Goodness to truth
- Post-conventional—The morality of non-violence[13]

Gilligan's theory can help us understand the importance of care in the moral development of students of both genders. Additionally, Gilligan's advocacy for non-violence can be an important topic for consideration and conversation as educators develop plans for classes, programming, and other co-curricular activities.

Transitions are key elements to understand within moral development theory. In light of the theories presented, Nancy Schlossberg's theory adds rich context to understanding the critical transitions experienced by college students. Schlossberg's theory delineates such transitions as any *event* or *non-event* that results in changes to relationships, routines, expectations, and roles. Transitions provide vital opportunities for development. How students assess the liabilities and assets associated with a given transition is critical. Schlossberg also suggests that students will assess their sense of marginality versus mattering. How a student assesses his/her mattering is directly connected to his/her sense of belonging.[14]

Schlossberg identifies three parts to the transition process:

- Approach Change—assessment of transition and its ramifications
- Take Stock—
  - *Situation*: understanding the circumstances of the transition
  - *Self*: understanding characteristics and demographics, awareness
  - *Support*: understanding the help that is available

- ○ *Strategies*: understanding how to deal or cope with transition
- Take Charge—taking control of the transition and making necessary changes[15]

Schlossberg's theory holds great significance for those who work with college students. The freshman transition to college is a crucial time for the development of students. Additionally, students will face numerous transitions throughout their time in college, culminating in graduation. Student-development educators can actively address the importance of transitions, considering programming options and/or devoting one-on-one time with students to help them take stock and take charge. Student development practitioners should also consider the importance of mattering versus marginality in a student's life, and how to foster mattering in their relationships with students.

Experiential Learning and Identity Development

Another essential element of understanding student development is the critical nature of experiential learning. David Kolb's theory of experiential learning helps us see the different ways that college students learn. Educators can use Kolb's theory to identify the learning styles of their students and challenge them to move through the cycle of learning stages, practicing different methods of learning. Kolb's theory of experiential learning presents four stages:

- Concrete experience (CE): Learner actively experiences something
- Reflective observation (RO): Learner consciously reflects on that experience
- Abstract conceptualization (AC): Learner conceptualizes a "theory" of what is observed
- Active experimentation (AE): Learner plans how to test theory

Learning is achieved as students move through these stages: *Feeling to Watching, Watching to Thinking, Thinking to Action.*[16]

Building on the foundation laid through Erik Erikson's work, James Marcia's identity development theory holds that identity is formed as people deal with *Crisis* and *Commitment*. Crisis is understood as a time of exploration and engagement with competing choices in different realms. Marcia identifies these realms as *Occupational, Religious*, and *Socio-political.*

According to Marcia, identity achievement is realized through status as one navigates crisis and commitment.[17] Marcia's theory presents four identity statuses:

- Identity Diffusion (no crisis/no commitment)
- Identity Foreclosure (no crisis/commitment)
- Identity Moratorium (crisis en route to commitment)
- Identity Achieved (post-crisis with personal commitments)

	No Commitment	Commitment
No Crisis	Identity Diffusion	Identity Foreclosure
Crisis	Identity Moratorium	Identity Achievement

In practically applying Marcia's theory, the encouraged deconstruction of presuppositions relating to occupational/vocational, religious, and socio-political realms can push students through successful navigation of crisis toward commitment and ultimately identity achievement.

Helping foreclosed students move toward identity achievement provides clarity and confidence in the midst of the influential years of college. The work associated with student development—especially the residence hall—can encourage growth and development toward commitment and identity realization.

Faith Development

The final developmental theories to be explored are those related to faith. James Fowler's faith development theory draws from the work of Erikson,

Piaget, and Kohlberg.[18] Fowler claims that faith development is critical as humans attempt to discover meaning in life.

Fowler posits that faith is ultimately a life commitment and not a single act. Fowler presents progressive stages:

- Prestage 1: Primal Faith
- Stage 1: Projective: Early childhood—Simple-faith
- Stage 2: Mythic-Literal: Middle-late childhood—Beginnings of internalization
- Stage 3: Synthetic-Conventional: Early adolescence— Internalization-identification
- Stage 4: Individuating-Reflective: Late adolescence/Early adult— Internalization
- Stage 5: Paradoxical-Consolidated: Middle adulthood— Sustaining
- Stage 6: Universalizing: Middle-late adulthood[19]

Spirituality is part of a holistic development of students. Fowler's theory is useful in emphasizing creating time for reflection and developing teaching methods that encourage students to assess their engagement and understanding of spirituality.

Sharon Daloz Parks' theory builds on the faith-development theory of Fowler in identifying a missing stage: young adulthood.[20] Parks posits that during young adulthood individuals develop life dreams. Parks describes a life dream as a fusion of strengths and passions in light of the needs of the world; embedded within is a strong emphasis on the need for students to have mentors. Mentors can challenge students to understand and articulate their faith and allow that faith to inform the fulfillment of life dreams.[21]

Parks' theory is not linear, but allows for the three forms of development to interact in the process of faith development:

- Forms of Knowing: Authority-bound, Unqualified Relativism, Probing Commitment, Tested Commitment, Convictional Commitment
- Forms of Dependence: Dependent/Counter-dependent, Fragile Inner Dependence, Confident Inner Dependence Interdependence
- Forms of Community: Conventional Community, Diffuse Community, Mentoring Community, Self-selected Group, Open to the Other[22]

Educators can foster faith development through the maturation of critical thinking skills. Furthermore, educators have the ability to encourage students toward the development of a life dream and aiding in the process of refining the motivation for that dream. All of this can be achieved through developing mentor/mentee relationships with students and investing significant time into individual students' faith development. This topic is developed more fully in chapter five.

Conclusion

Star Trek captured the imagination of its audience by creating innovative imagery that raised the question of technology's *telos* or end. The idea of boldly going where no man has gone before is deeply entrenched in the hearts of the students who step onto campuses all across the diverse landscape of higher education.

In similar fashion, Apple's[23] advertisement for selling its 2014 iteration of the iPad borrows from Walt Whitman: "That you are here—that life exists and identity—that the powerful play goes on and you may contribute a verse . . . that the powerful play goes on and you may contribute a verse . . . What will your verse be?"[24] The repeated haunting conclusion aims beyond imagining the future of technology. Rather, its powerful imagery directs the hearts of its audience back to the common ground at the root of human existence and, in turn, the impetus for student development: students' pursuit of purpose.

Step into the classroom or courtyard of any modern campus and you will undoubtedly see this product and its many Apple likenesses in the hands of droves of students. While the product has been successfully marketed, the sense of calling and purpose embedded in the ad is a more difficult message to convey.

Reflecting on his experience as a concentration-camp inmate, Viktor Frankl (1992) wrote in 1946: "Man's search for meaning is the primary motivation in his life."[25] That form of pursuit captures well the mission of higher education, student development, and residential life. Behind the oceans of iPads and iPhones are young men and women in pursuit of purpose, and the job of higher education is to inculcate it in students' lives. The powerful play goes on and each one contributes a verse.

DISCUSSION QUESTIONS

Take a few moments and answer the questions. Jot down some of your thoughts under the questions for further discussion with the staff.

1. What is the value of applying development theory to work in residence-life?

2. Are there specific aspects of the theories presented that seem more applicable to the students with whom you work?

3. What stages of identity development resonate with your college experience? Are there other elements of the theories that ring true with your development in college?

4. What forms of active roles—within the theories presented—can you take as an RA in helping the students with whom you work?

ACTIVITIES

1. Develop programming ideas for your floors around the seven vectors presented by Chickering. Example: What kind of programming might you create to help students toward *developing mature interpersonal relationships*?

2. Implement Schlossberg's transition theory in considering the experiences of freshmen and seniors.

3. What would the "mentoring community" that Parks suggests look like on your campus?

4. Discuss: How do you inspire students to pursue meaning and purpose in the midst of everything else that clamors for their attention?

CHAPTER 4

The Role of the Resident Assistant in Developing a Community

More Than Just Getting Along

Kristin Hansen Keiffer, Amy Van Der Werf and Doug Wood

It's the start of the academic year. Kayleigh and Allison are two new roommates, each sitting on their freshly made beds in their quiet room. They are texting their friends from back home and barely acknowledging one another's presence. The silence is awkward and lonely. It is their first night in the room, having just moved in to start orientation earlier that day. Although Kayleigh and Allison befriended each other via Facebook in the summer after receiving their housing assignment, actually communicating in person is turning out to be difficult. It seems they're much more at ease negotiating relationships digitally. At times, they wonder, "Should I text her?" just to break the ice.

Soon their RA Eliza pops her head in their door and invites them to a floor ice-breaker activity. They spend the next hour with their floor-mates doing crazy get-to-know-you games strategically designed to learn names and foster a shared experience. It works. Along with their new floor-mates, amidst smiles and growing laughter, Allison and Kayleigh have hit it off, and they open up to each other and the possibilities of the new semester.

Created for Community

The importance of community stems from our creation. In Genesis it is a relational, triune God who lovingly forms man from the dust and imprints the divine image within him. From this relational God we understand that the original design is for harmony with God and the creation. The Lord pronounced his entire handiwork as "good" or "very good," with the exception of Adam's loneliness, which he knew was "not good."[1] God did not make us to live alone in isolation. The shipwrecked Chuck Noland, a character played by Tom Hanks in the 1998 movie "Cast Away," provides a good example. To stave off insanity, Chuck crafts an imaginary friend, Wilson, out of a volleyball that washed up in the cargo from his downed plane. Without Wilson, Noland wouldn't have survived.[2]

As a resident assistant, fostering a safe and nurturing living environment is critical for promoting a sense of belonging. Community grows as relationships deepen. But just how do you promote these relationships? What is the ideal vision for community at a college? How does community develop and flourish?

Building Community

American educator Ernest L. Boyer was a stalwart advocate for building strong and vibrant communities on college campuses. In *Campus Life: In Search of Community*, Boyer expounded on problematic student behaviors which can impede the fulfillment of educational mission. Alcohol abuse, lack of civility, and sexual and racial harassment are cited as real challenges at institutions of higher learning, requiring fresh approaches to building community. Boyer called for communities of higher learning to be *purposeful, open, just, disciplined, caring and celebrative*.[3] The resident assistant has an important role in fostering elements of Boyer's ideals for campus life.

Residents living in community should never lose sight of *why* they are in college. Yet, this too often happens. Students emboldened by new freedoms find their new purpose in social outlets often at the expense of attending class. Many students are burdened with financial concerns and some will work excessively while neglecting their studies. Lack of self-care and sleep combined with the stress of project deadlines and exams commonly lead to physical and mental fatigue. Students too easily lose their way. Boyer calls for campuses to be educationally *purposeful*—places "where faculty and students share academic goals and work together to strengthen teaching and learning on campus."[4] Your role as an RA is critical in helping keep your residents mindful of their academic goals.

Residents also need assurance that the spaces they inhabit, both in and outside the classroom, are *open* spaces "where freedom of expression is uncompromisingly protected and where civility is powerfully affirmed."[5] Balancing free expression and civility is both delicate and necessary. The RA who challenges and inspires her residents to consider others—their values, beliefs, passions, even questions—and listens well, inculcates genuine understanding and healthy relationships in the community. Pay attention to posters, room and door decorations, and other venues of student expression, including social media. Is there anything offensive? What are the teachable moments? Will all students feel welcome in your community?

Ernest Boyer also calls for communities of higher education to be *just* places "where the sacredness of the person is honored and where diversity is aggressively pursued."[6] Most colleges and universities today have noble goals to enroll students from diverse backgrounds. Education is considered excellent when inclusivity and diversity are present. Graduates who have achieved a high level of intercultural competency are highly desired in our globalized economy. We'll have more on this subject in another chapter on the "The RA's role with diversity."

More and more students from underrepresented populations, children of immigrant families, and students who are the first in their family to attend college are matriculating—and rightly so. Yet on most campuses, these students remain in the minority. What is the experience of the students living in your section for whom English is not the first language? How comfortable are the only African Americans living in your residence hall? How attuned are your ears to micro-aggressive utterances such as "that's so gay" or "I was jewed"? As a resident assistant, you are tasked with promoting endless welcome to students from all backgrounds. Be inspired to know their stories and vigorously protect all students, especially those who have been traditionally marginalized. Walk in their shoes and seek their wisdom. Students learn the most from their peers. How you model hospitality and foster inclusivity can make or break a student's experience.

Most institutions of higher learning promote standards of conduct to ensure that the learning environment is maintained. A *disciplined* community is a "place where individuals accept their obligations to the group and where well-defined governance procedures guide behavior for the common good."[7] Ideally, a committee comprised of students, administrators, trustee members, educators, and staff, meets regularly to create, review, revise and communicate these important statutes and articulate a clear rationale. It's your responsibility as an RA to know, help communicate, model, and assist in upholding these standards.

Enforcement of these policies is another important role of the RA in promoting a disciplined community. While often viewed as challenging, holding your residents accountable for their misbehavior helps reinforce the educational community and promotes stability and cohesion. Students living in your section should not only know the rules, but the reasons for the rules. Don't just post floor "quiet hours." Explain why unruly commotion impedes scholarship. Be articulate about the advantages of drug-and alcohol-free living environments. Teach the benefits of the policies encouraging a mutual commitment to "the common good."

When behavior occurs that disrupts learning, an RA should be equipped to confront students appropriately. You should always seek to respect students who have behaved poorly and made bad decisions. Call to mind their value as a child of God. Stay in close contact with your more seasoned Residence Director when confronting misbehavior and strive to maintain a good relationship with residents who get in trouble. Trust that the student conduct procedures will allow for redemptive correction, accountability, and restoration to the community. Be prepared to walk alongside your resident during this process.

A *caring* community is a place "where the well-being of each member is sensitively supported and where service to others is encouraged."[8] Taking a genuine interest in the lives of each of your residents helps students feel connected to you and, by extension, to your campus. Promoting a culture of caring among your residents will aid in their being connected to one another. Knowing they belong is a critical predictor of whether or not a student will graduate. Building bonds among your residents will foster safety, inclusion, and well-being. Establishing a floor prayer chain, hosting open room dialogues, listening well to life stories, and practicing hospitality are just some of the ways the RA can help to establish a caring community.

Most residents will have affiliations with other campus groups as well. Their interests will vary from playing varsity soccer to acting in a theater production, from leading the Anime Club to serving as treasurer for the Psychology Club. These disparate sub-groups often live under one roof. Helping residents discover their commonality and pursue friendship amidst differences is important in building community.

Ernest Boyer speaks further about the need for students to make a connection between what they learn and how they live. He encourages efforts to help all students see beyond themselves and understand their responsibility to the larger community.

> We are especially concerned that students reach out to others—to children and to older people to build bridges across the generations. Students also should be brought in touch with those genuinely in need, and through field experiences, build relationships that are intergenerational, intercultural, and international, too. In the end, the campus should be viewed not only as a place of introspection, but also as a staging ground for action.[9]

The RA can assist in planning and encouraging residents to participate in community-service projects and other volunteer opportunities. Ideally, the floor community should be a place where students can grapple with how their education can contribute to society and impact humanity.

Finally, Boyer calls on the campus to be a *celebrative* community, where "the heritage of the institution is remembered and where rituals affirming both tradition and change are widely shared."[10] The heritage of your college or university must be honored and its traditions embraced for community to flourish on your campus. It's your role as an RA to learn the unique history of your college mission and heritage. In the same way, you should know and pass along the story of your residence. How did your residence hall or apartment section get its name? What do you know about the person or people for whom the hall is named? What memories, special stories, and traditions have been given shape to its unique history? How are you passing this knowledge along?

Just as your college hosts the rituals of orientation, convocation, and commencement, so too should meaningful rites and celebrations be enmeshed in the fabric of your residential community. If there are little to no traditions in your residence, work with your Residence Director to create them or to breathe new life into existing ones. They should be lively, safe, inclusive, and unifying. The challenge is to install rituals and ceremonies with real significance—and fun as well.

Stages of Community

Understanding the ideal principles of community on a college campus provides a vision of what to strive for as a resident assistant. Having knowledge of the stages of community will give focus to that vision. The start of the academic year will be different for the various residential communities on campus. One living area may have quite a head start because most of the upper-class residents already know each other from previous years. Simultaneously, another group of new students may be starting from scratch. Even though these communities are unique in their make-up, they share common characteristics. Scott Peck in *A Different Drummer* describes four stages of community making that groups routinely go through. The stages of community building identified by Peck include *pseudocommunity, chaos, emptiness,* and *community*.[11] Every group will not follow this paradigm exactly, but this process of community making is the natural order of things.

According to Peck, the first stage in community building is *pseudocommunity*. It is often the initial response of group members to attempt to form community quickly by being overly nice with one another and avoiding any type of conflict.[12] Think back to the first time you lived with your college roommate or roommates. Do you remember how kind you were when you first met? You were most likely very slow in sharing your true feelings about the Disney princess posters and hoped you would just "get used to them"? You may have been the one to do the dishes every single night for the first week without saying a word, even humming "make me a servant" as you dried the coffee mug and put it back in the cupboard. You didn't voice your disagreements. You let things slide. You were super nice. They were super nice. You were avoiding conflict and living in pseudocommunity. From the outside it may have seemed you were establishing a stress-free and pleasant living arrangement. But this wasn't authentic community. True community involves communicating honestly and civilly and working to resolve conflict. While pseudocommunity is not ideal, it is necessary for students new to a living area and just starting the journey to true community.

Chaos is Peck's second stage. Moving into this phase can seem frightening for students but is necessary in order to emerge from the shallowness of pseudo community. Instead of trying to ignore or hide differences or frustrations, community members begin to put them out in the open in an attempt to see change. The motive behind this openness is the hope that others will like them. The chaos stage is filled with struggle and generally is not fun. As an RA, you will see chaos come more quickly when communities are in close proximity. Roommate conflicts occur before conflicts on the broader living area emerge. Chaos is not necessarily a bad place for your residents. Conflict is better than pretending when there is division because it's more authentic. It's a difficult stage but there is hope that you will move beyond it.[13]

The next stage of community building is *emptiness*. In the chaos stage there are two options: one is to remain as individuals and separate from community altogether; the other is to move into and through the emptiness with the other members of the group. Peck lists common barriers to communication that residents need to push through before entering into true community. These include: expectations and preconceptions; prejudice; ideology, theology and solutions; the need to heal, convert, fix or solve; and the need to control. Emptiness is a time of sacrifice. This sacrifice hurts because it is a death to self and necessitates rebirth. The emptiness stage takes a lot of effort for the community members to wrestle through. Unlike the self-centered chaos stage, which is marked by the need to be liked, emptiness involves working to process conflict selflessly for the benefit of the group. Your residents have the most to gain from you as an RA during this phase as you encourage them to consider the value of their community and commit themselves to working through these barriers.

The final stage is *true community*. After the pain and death of the emptiness stage, there is a peace that follows that includes a new kind of openness and vulnerability. This is the true community stage, where residents entrust themselves to deeper, more authentic, and more harmonious relationships. Residential communities that have reached this stage are characterized by openness, consideration for others, and enjoyment of trusted friendships achieved through the earlier stages.

Inclusivity in Community

We know from recent research that diverse educational environments are critical to attaining excellent and holistic learning. The American Council on Education has stated the importance of diversity in higher education.[14]

- Diversity enriches the educational experience. We learn from those whose experiences, beliefs, and perspectives are different from our own, and these lessons can be taught best in a richly diverse intellectual and social environment.
- It promotes personal growth—and a healthy society. Diversity challenges stereotyped preconceptions; it encourages critical

thinking; and it helps students learn to communicate effectively with people of varied backgrounds.

- It strengthens communities and the workplace. Education within a diverse setting prepares students to become good citizens in an increasingly complex, pluralistic society; it fosters mutual respect and teamwork; and it helps build communities whose members are judged by the quality of their character and their contributions.

- It enhances America's economic competitiveness. Sustaining the nation's prosperity in the 21st century will require us to make effective use of the talents and abilities of all our citizens, in work settings that bring together individuals from diverse backgrounds and cultures.[15]

Many colleges and universities are striving to recruit students from diverse cultures and experiences to enhance the learning that can occur on campus. This increased diversity in campus residences provides students the opportunity to learn how to thrive and grow with people who may have very different perspectives and experiences. These perspectives are shaped by the culture that a student experienced prior to coming to college. The culture we experience plays a significant role in shaping our views, our values, what we think is funny, what we are loyal to, what we worry about, and what we fear. If you are from southern California or Tennessee, if you grew up with a single parents or grandparents, if you were Baptist, Catholic, or Pentecostal, you will see the world in a particular way. In building healthy living areas in the college residences, it is important for RAs to have an understanding of or at least sensitivity to these differences, but also find ways for students to connect through their common experiences.

Certainly most first-year students, regardless of the culture they come from, experience some anxiety around coming to college. Most students are trying to determine a major and a direction for their lives. Finding ways to help students connect around these commonalties will promote a sense of inclusion and belonging. (The topic of inclusion and diversity is more fully developed in Chapter Six.)

The RA faces an important challenge in helping students find common ground, while at the same time recognizing and honoring differences. It is important in building community that you not pretend that differences don't exist, but rather value the experience and culture of each student.

Consider the words of James 2:1–7, as rendered in The Message:[16]

1-4 My dear friends, don't let public opinion influence how you live out our glorious, Christ-originated faith. If a man enters your church wearing an expensive suit, and a street person wearing rags comes in right after him, and you say to the man in the suit, "Sit here, sir; this is the best seat in the house!" and either ignore the street person or say, "Better sit here in the back row," haven't you segregated God's children and proved that you are judges who can't be trusted?

5-7 Listen, dear friends. Isn't it clear by now that God operates quite differently? He chose the world's down-and-out as the kingdom's first citizens, with full rights and privileges. This kingdom is promised to anyone who loves God. And here you are abusing these same citizens! Isn't it the high and mighty who exploit you, who use the courts to rob you blind? Aren't they the ones who scorn the new name—"Christian"—used in your baptisms?

In this passage, a host gives a better seat at the table to those with culturally valued characteristics and a worse seat to the poor man who did not have what was valued in society. As an RA, you should strive to be Christlike and ensure that every person has a valued seat at your table.

The Influence of Technology on Community

It is important for RAs to be aware of the influence technology, specifically social media, has on community. Facebook, Twitter, YouTube and countless other forms of social media are avenues for us to engage in community. In some ways these provide great opportunities to make connections with others, but there must be an awareness of how they can hinder community as well.

Positive Influences on Community

By the time students get to campus, many of them have already connected with others in their class via Facebook and other social media platforms. Most college housing offices encourage new roommates to share their digital information with each other ahead of time. This initial introduction can help students converse and find points of connection, so when residents finally meet each other face to face, they already have a head start.

RAs benefit from social media in similar ways. Mining the Facebook pages of your residents for interesting nuggets helps them know you care about them and their story. If you can memorize one or two tidbits—from "you have a dog named Molly" to "you were drum major for your high-school marching band"—they will feel encouraged that you care. As the year progresses, social media will remain a useful medium to share information about programs, student activities, and other campus events and provide one avenue (of many) for dialogue and discussion.

Challenges to Community

Of course, early connections via social media are only as authentic as the person who shares. Some students hide behind the façade of social media and create a "desired" self, rather than express who they really are. They feel more comfortable living behind the screen and are uncomfortable in face-to-face situations. Students can also create uncivil and crass communication via social media because of the anonymity it provides. As an RA, it will be important for you to use technology as a means to enhance community, and determine when it is best to have in-person conversations and activities.

Tips
- Keep a healthy balance of online communication with in-person interactions
- Don't interact with others online differently than you would in person (i.e. don't say something to them online you wouldn't say in person.)
- When it's appropriate, check in with your residents in cyberspace, especially if they are difficult to connect with in person. But, be sure this isn't your only means of communication.

Now What? The Role of an RA in Community Development

As a resident assistant, you play a vital role in helping to build community among the residents assigned to you. Understanding your students need for authentic community and embracing the ideals of community on a college campus is a meaningful framework upon which to build. Here are some ways you can help to create community on your floor:

Identify a Purpose

Students can often forget why they are attending college. In order for a community to thrive, it is essential for there to be a common goal or purpose. You should begin by identifying what the purpose is for your living-area community. There may be aspects of this purpose that are prescribed by your institution, but there may also be some flexibility for you to influence part of this purpose. As referenced earlier, Ernest Boyer suggests that campuses should be places "where faculty and students share academic goals and work together to strengthen teaching and learning on campus."[17]

Be Open and Available

Community starts with connecting residents one at a time. You will play a significant role in the early stages of this development. Being present and available for your residents is especially critical during this early phase. Planning strategies to connect students to one another and establishing a vision for your community will be meaningful and helpful. After fostering initial "get to know you" activities, in the days and weeks that follow, leave your door open, post your schedule, and spend time. The relationships you build will help to establish the caring community Boyer espouses.

Create Shared Experiences

One way community forms is through shared experiences. These can be formal engagements, such as floor meetings or programs that you plan, or they can be informal experiences such as conversations in the hallway. Many residences have traditions that provide ideal opportunities for community building. Also remember Ernest Boyer's call to give back to the college or local community by planning and performing service projects together. As an RA you should intentionally utilize these opportunities for residents to spend time together and create memories to work toward deep community.

Be Inclusive in Community Building

The importance of creating a welcoming and inclusive space for all residents cannot be overstated. A very simple way to promote inclusion is through providing opportunities for students to share their stories. Strategize in advance how you can accomplish this, either through regular gatherings or other initiatives designed to foster purposeful dialogue. (A popular residence-life program is the weekly "Chai Chat" storytelling series.) Always seek to have residents' stories affirmed and encourage good listening and respectful question-and-answer time.

Consider the Physical Space

How warm and inviting is the space you share with your residents? Some campus housing was designed specifically to foster community within an aesthetically comfortable and welcoming space. A simple way to make the students feel more at home is by adding door decorations and providing unique décor in the lounge. Unfortunately, many campuses have much older, more utilitarian residences. These were constructed block and mortar style in the middle of the twentieth century for former soldiers going to college on the GI bill. Resembling more of a barracks than learning space, they were blueprinted with little thought for community. If you and your residents inherit such a space, try your best to transform it as you are able. Work with your RD and facilities staff to warm up the space. Sometimes life together in an older celebrated living space becomes a shared experience which powerfully contributes to the community in its own way.

Remember the Stages of Community Development

In his article "The Outward Bounds 'Temporary Community': A Practical Framework for Understanding Residence Life," Eric Spiecker provides resident assistants with a practical approach for remembering and accommodating Scott Speck's stages of community.[18] He interprets these stages like this:

- *Getting Acquainted* (Time frame: beginning of academic year–end of September). This is Peck's pseudo community stage, a starting point in new relationships oozing with niceties and conflict avoidance. During this time your residents will be patient with each other, they want to be included, they want others to take an interest in them, and in general there will be good feelings throughout your section. This could easily be called the honeymoon phase of life together. As an RA, during this time you'll want to create places for residents to get to learn each other's names, be sure there are places for trust and openness, and be sure everyone is included.
- *Struggling Forward* (Time frame: October–November). Struggling forward is another way to view Peck's chaos phase. This is the season where roommate conflicts surface, where residents begin to voice frustration over certain community policies or complaints about the physical plant. It's the time

in the semester when many class assignments or projects come due, and mid-term exams approach. The increased stress of coursework coupled with less tolerance of roommates' or floor-mates' idiosyncrasies promotes higher levels of dissatisfaction and conflict. As an RA you need to be attuned and responsive to this. You may see divisions, jealousy, gossip, and hurt feelings in this season. While this is challenging, remember that the authenticity which accompanies the tension is necessary for true community to be developed. As an RA, seek to create safe places for your residents to move beyond superficiality and to struggle together. Listen well. Model healthy communication and intervene when necessary.

- *Becoming Personal* (Time frame: December–middle of February). Emptiness is how Peck describes this phase of becoming personal; it is characterized by residents displaying increased levels of vulnerability and discomfort with living in community.[19] While it can be initially frightening, encourage residents to take attention off themselves and consider the needs of others. This emptying of self and one's own desires is necessary to move through the stages of community. As an RA, you will want to provide support for residents as they grapple with self-denial. You should seek ways to promote healing and reconciliation among residents, especially for relationships that are damaged during this time. Again, pay attention to the needs of your residents during this phase. Be quick to foster dialogue and open communication. Also look for support from your residence director and other seasoned professionals within the residence-life department.
- *Working Together* (Time frame: middle of February–April). After negotiating the challenges of the previous stages of community, you and your residents should be able to realize the more harmonious season of what Eric Spiecker calls "working

together."[20] This season aligns with Peck's True Community stage and is characterized by openness, trust, caring for others, willingness to sacrifice, and displays of grace. Living in this phase should be a fruitful and peaceful experience as you and your residents come to value their identity in community. You may even see a reduction in your leadership responsibilities as you help your residents reflect on their prior struggles, realize their own potential, and enjoy their friendships.

- *Saying Good-Bye* (Time frame: May–end of term). The community formed in your living area is a temporary community. There is an intentional beginning and ending time for this unique group of individuals. You will notice that your residents will have mixed emotions as they prepare to say good bye to their community. As an RA, you will want to provide opportunities for closure, listen to students who are sad or concerned about leaving, celebrate the growth and change that has been experienced throughout the year, and plan with them for the future. Even though emotions during this final phase may be bittersweet, take the time to share memories and celebrate accomplishments. We hope that the journey through the academic year together has been seasoned with personal and spiritual growth and the achievement of academic goals.

Conclusion

As a resident assistant, your role in building community on your floor is crucial. The work you undertake to foster a welcoming and safe learning environment will greatly impact your residents' undergraduate experience and ultimately contribute to their personal growth and the fulfillment of their academic aspirations. It will be helpful for you to understand our created need for community, the ideal principles of community on our college campus, and the stages in their development as you help create the kind of living space you desire for your residents.

DISCUSSION QUESTIONS

Take a few moments and answer the questions. Jot down some of your thoughts for further discussion with the staff.

1. Can you think of a time you were isolated from others? How did this feel?

2. What reflections do you have about God's design for his creation to live in community?

3. What principles of community from Boyer will be more challenging to incorporate as you build community in your residence?

4. Rank your students on Peck's community development stages. How would you describe your campus climate relative to the experience of students from underrepresented populations? What about the climate in your specific living area? In what ways has diversity enhanced your education in college?

5. Do you have any examples of how technology has negatively affected the community in your living area?

Application

1. What are some strategies you can incorporate on your floor to help you reach these ideals?

2. How have you used technology to enhance the community in your living area?

3. What are some additional ways you promote inclusivity in your living area?

4. Explore the entire living area using the chapter's concepts and consider how you can move your residents closer to true community.

CHAPTER 5

The Role of the Resident Assistant
in Faith Development

The Big Question about Doubt

Stephen Beers

Think back over the past week. Isn't it true that many students in your residence were thinking about, asking, or discussing significant spiritual questions? The questions being raised may have been generated by a discussion in a science class about how God created the world or a topic presented in a Bible class that challenged their understanding of how to interpret scripture. Maybe the spiritual question surfaced after a student's first personal encounter with a homeless person which led to thoughts about God's character, human will, and responsibility. These spiritual questions, coupled with the ensuing dialogue, probe at the meaning of life and faith.

The college years are a unique time in life when big questions are asked and answers are owned. College students feel a sense of urgency in seeking answers to big questions, perhaps for the first time. They are drawn with a resolve to figure out who they are, what they believe, and eventually to live their lives accordingly. Questions and experiences shape what one discusses. What one discusses eventually forms one's understanding. These constructed and organized ideas then influence one's values and eventually direct one's practices. Therefore, the college years are critical years in shaping people for the future. Partnering with faculty and staff, Christian college RAs are in an amazing position to lead and direct worthy conversations and practical experiences that facilitate the faith development of their residents.

Scripture imparts a calling upon every believer to be a spiritual leader. Jesus, as he is about to depart from this earth, finishes a conversation with the disciples that is fitting to a Christian RA's leadership role:

> Therefore, go and make disciples of all nations, baptizing them
> in the name of the Father and of the Son and of the Holy Spirit
> and teaching them to obey everything I have commanded you.
> (Matthew 28:19-20a)[1]

As a spiritual leader in your living community, you are called to train and instruct those you meet in the ways of Christ. As an RA, your role as a spiritual leader in the faith development of your residents is an outgrowth of your larger calling as a follower of Christ.

One of the biggest challenges of being a "spiritual peer leader" in a small living community is navigating leadership in ways that balance vulnerability with being authentic and appropriate. To be sure, peer leaders are often asking the same big questions and often struggling to establish their own appropriate spiritual practices. So, before getting into the nuts and bolts of faith development, here are two encouraging thoughts. First, at the end of this chapter you will find some time-honored applications to assist you in the practical day-to-day spiritual leadership role. Second, remember that our God is a gracious God who fully understands your situation and your limitations. Christ does not expect you to be a spiritual leader alone, as exemplified by his final words to his disciples before his return to heaven in Matthew 28:20: "I am with you always to the very end of the age."[2]

The rest of the chapter is organized into three sections: the "what," the "so what" and the "now what." The "what" section discusses information and theory of faith development. The "so what" portion outlines why this information is relevant to the RA. And last, the "now what" provides practical application.

The "What": Understanding Faith Development Theory

To succeed as a spiritual leader, it is essential for you to have a basic understanding of the process of spiritual formation. The apostle Paul states in Romans12:1–2 that a person is transformed by the renewing of his mind. In other words, what one thinks makes all the difference. Therefore, before overviewing faith-development theory, it will be helpful to explore what psychology has taught us about the mental changes that occur to students during the college years.

The Connection between Faith Development and Identity Development

The college years have been dubbed "the critical years" because it is during this period that one's identity is formed. As we saw in an earlier chapter, Erick Erickson, the preeminent developmental psychologist, suggested that the developmental role of college-aged, emerging adults is the formation of their identity. What he means by this is that young people must define who they are and how they will fit into the larger societal structure (i.e. personality strengths, vocational choices). Also recall Arthur Chickering's description of how individuals develop in seven distinct ways (vectors): achieving competence, managing emotions, becoming autonomous, establishing identity, freeing interpersonal relationships, developing a purpose, and developing integrity.[3] These developmental tasks provide a quick yet full overview of what is transpiring in the lives of college students. This means that college students are finding out their preferences and competencies, separating from their family, and beginning to manage their personal relationships. Ultimately, they are weaving all of these changes together in order to answer the central questions that shape their beliefs, meaning, and purpose.

To understand how young people develop and accept their new identity, we can look at another developmental theorist who bridges the gap between human-developmental theory and faith-development theory. James Marcia outlines four identity "statuses" that can be used to gauge and illustrate a student's identity developmental position. Marcia suggests that all of us find ourselves in one of following four statuses:[4]

- *Identity Diffusion.* In this status, the individual does not have a sense of having choices about belief or values; he or she has not yet made nor is attempting/willing to make a commitment about who they are or what they believe. Here students are not even asking the tough questions nor entering into meaningful dialogue. Some have dubbed this stage the "whatever" stage because the student answers life's tough questions with "whatever."

- *Identity Foreclosure.* In this status the individual seems willing to commit to some relevant roles, values, and goals for the future. The student may have clear commitments, but those beliefs have not been tested. Most of these students hold other people's expectations and beliefs (i.e. those of parents) instead of authentically exploring a range of options for themselves. They have not experienced any significant identity crisis in which questions or experiences have challenged what they believe. In a study done by the Coalition of Christian Colleges and Universities in 1999,[5] it was found that 85 percent of CCCU freshmen were in this stage.

- *Identity Moratorium.* In this status the individual is currently in a crisis. She is exploring various commitments and is ready to make choices, but has not yet made a commitment. The crisis of belief may have come about through an event in his life or some new idea that has conflicted with his understanding of the world. That event could be as significant as a loved one being diagnosed with cancer or a different way to interpret scripture being presented by a trusted professor. A crisis of faith does not have to be a large event, but it must thrust the student into a state of non-resolution.

- *Identity Achievement.* This status is characterized by the individual having gone through an identity crisis and made a commitment to an aspect of a chosen identity (i.e. certain role or value). Here the student has exited the "crisis" and taken the time to authentically reorganize or accept a certain belief or practice. During four short college years, it is difficult to move fully into identity achievement.

As one can see from these descriptions, the students in your living area can be asking vastly different questions about life and faith. And, in fact, if they are "identity diffused," they may not be asking any questions at all. Marcia's theory brings to light that students' responses to a particular question or event are driven in part by where they are at in their own identity development. This means that crisis, questions, and doubt can eventually help facilitate an authentic ownership of a particular belief. Marcia maintains that without such a "crisis" there will not be real ownership.

Practically speaking, this means that some of your students will not be interested in engaging in "important" dialogue, while for others this dialogue may be the most important conversation that they have had in their life. Furthermore, their desire to find authentic answers to these questions is actually a redirecting experience. Take for example a student who is wondering for the first time if God is really a loving God as she has been taught all her life. This questioning may have been initiated by the "crisis" of a loved one being diagnosed with a terminal illness or by witnessing the devastation of a natural disaster. These real questions and "owned" answers provide teachable moments. These moments, which are more easily spotted in a living community, have the potential for helping the student understand how a loving God can let evil happen, eventually deepening faith, developing her identity, and influencing her practice.

An Overview of Faith-Development Theory

We have established that college is a critical time of changes in a young person's identity. These shifts are brought about in part through the many questions individuals asks of themselves, including questions of faith and belief. We could delve into a wide variety of faith development theories; but one particular faith developmental theorist's work may be especially helpful to you as a peer spiritual leader. James Loder developed a theory showing that faith develops through five positions: *contradiction, interlude for scanning, constructive act of imagination, opening, and reinterpretation.* Loder saw faith development in the context of "transformational moments" in which people develop faith as they confront new and challenging situations. The following are short descriptions and illustrations of each of the five positions:[6]

- *Contradiction.* Here the student's untested belief is challenged by what seems like new and contradictory information. This contradiction forces the student into a restless state. Let's return to our earlier example of finding out about a loved one who is gravely ill. The classic contradiction here for Christians is that they have been taught that God is a loving God, which now seems in great contrast to the experienced pain and suffering of this world. The preeminent question for the student now is "Why would a loving God allow my mother to suffer this way?"
- *Interlude for Scanning.* In this position the student enters a contemplative state of searching for potential answers. Like Marcia's "identity moratorium" the student is in crisis but has not made any decisions. In our example the student begins to look for and collect reasonable answers to the central question, "How can a loving God allow for suffering in this world?" Potential answers arise: "Well, maybe there really is no God at all or he is not able to act," "Maybe God is not good," "Maybe God is not a personal god and therefore cannot really care about me as an individual," "Maybe God has given us free will and that free will means there

is evil in this broken world and that God will mercifully and fully restore all of his children in the end"; or "God uses suffering in redemptive ways."

- *Constructive Act of Imagination*. Now the student begins to reconstruct a faithful answer that meets both of her criteria: a plausible theoretical construct and an answer that works in real life. Here the student is entering a transition period. In our example, the student begins to weigh out and assess all of the plausible answers. She assesses each one and may make reconstructive statements like, "I know God is real because I have experienced him in various ways." Or she may rhetorically ask foundational questions like, "Without a God what then is the meaning of life or our purpose?" For the Christian, scripture contains answers to many of these questions. With these authentic questions and dialogue, she begins then to construct a new, more resilient and pliable faith.

- *Opening*. Student in this position are now open to seeing their beliefs in a new way. Those who are unable to move into this open position remain in a state of flux or "moratorium," as outlined in Marcia's work. Students are now receptive to a reinterpretation of their belief. The new faith position incudes this new information, so that students are able to reconcile the "contradiction." Students make final tests of what are now newly constructed beliefs. So for example, the students begin to understand and are open to accepting that this world is broken and that God's redemptive work is not finished in the short span that each human lives on the earth. God has a purpose in allowing evil and brokenness for a time and suffering can be used for good.

- *Reinterpretation*. In this last step, students own the new faith perspective, and there is a stabilization of belief. They have more fully constructed and owned the new understanding of how God can be good and allow evil in this world. They have accepted that "God's perfect will is at work in the brokenness and his restorative mercy will in the end expose his true good nature."[7]

We do not have space to include a full review of James Fowler's theory of faith development, but a brief exposure to his work may be helpful for this conversation. Fowler proposes six distinct stages of faith. During the college years, most students, he postulates, are in one of two developmental transitions: either a time where "faith must synthesize values and information and . . . provide a basis for identity and outlook" or a later stage where "the student must take seriously the burden of responsibility for his own commitments, lifestyle, beliefs and attitudes."[8] As you can see, the students we are working with are in a position to be asking tough questions and making life-defining decisions about who they are and how they will live.

As we have seen, faith development is inseparable from what one believes and thinks. But faith, especially in the context of a Christian experience, is also inseparable from practice and action. The Apostle Paul speaks of faith without works being dead, and scripture consistently suggests that one can know about someone's faith by their "fruit." Benson and Eklin, who are Christian faith development researchers, have constructed a holistic-faith-developmental assessment tool that provides insight. Their eight dimensions of practical Christian faith development are tied to specific outcomes of maturing faithful Christians.[9] The eight dimensions are:

1. *Trusts in God's saving grace and believes firmly in the humanity and divinity of Jesus*
2. *Experiences a sense of personal well-being, security, and peace*
3. *Integrates faith and life, seeing work, family, social relationships, and political choices as part of one's religious life*
4. *Seeks spiritual growth through study, reflection, prayer, and discussion with others*

5. *Seeks to be a part of a community of believers in which people give witness to their faith and support and nourish one another*
6. *Holds life-affirming values including commitment to racial and gender equality, affirmation of cultural and religious diversity, and a personal sense of responsibility for the welfare of others*
7. *Advocates social and global change to bring about greater social justice*
8. *Serves humanity, consistently and passionately, through acts of love and justice*

The college years are the years in which students ask big questions and begin to own the answers. Those answers ultimately shape their future. As the RA, you have the opportunity to be a part of this conversation and help shape the student's identity. Later in the chapter, you will find this eight-point list paired with illustrations for practical applications of faith development activities.

The "So what": Implications of Faith Development Theory

It may be helpful to spend some time answering the question "So what?" or "What does all this faith-development theorizing really mean to me as an RA?" Although these theoretical narratives are helpful in gaining a big picture understanding of what is happening, they may not be practical enough to give direction to an RA during a midnight conversation with a student in "crisis." Nor do these theories necessarily provide specific implications for RAs attempting to do faith development programing in the first three weeks of the semester. The following insights are provided to build a conceptual bridge between a theoretical construct of faith stages and the real lives of those living in a college community.

The Process of Faith Development Is Full of Authentic Questions, Searching, and Doubt

For a student to be authentic in asking good questions and genuinely searching for answers, there must be a component of doubt. In this context, doubt benefits faith development because it forces us to look hard at what we believe and how that belief works in the real world. The Old Testament psalmists are encouraging writers for those of us in doubt, as their scripts are full of real people asking relevant and difficult questions. These real-life examples of spiritual journeys help lead us into owning the mysterious and sometime confusing aspects of our own faith. Doubt and faith are not mutually exclusive. Doubt is not a sign of weakness but a sign of growth that forces us to look at who we think God is. Authentic questions, searching, and doubt are the exercises to a deeper and more vibrant faith.

Faith development will include some crisis. All faith development theories suggest that crisis is an excellent initiator of change. This may come as a surprise and in some way be disheartening. But when one thinks more clearly about it, crisis provides an unparalleled opportunity to review what one believes and how one acts. In the crucible of crisis, people test their assumptions against real world experiences. This means that RAs should not be fearful of crisis or attempt to shield students from difficult experiences. With support, encouragement, and hope, crises can be traversed and become a positive influence in students' faith development.

Faith development is ultimately about transition. If at the end of a student's time in college she is not a different person, then the college faculty and staff have not done their job. Developing a stronger faith means changing. For example, if a college student enters the institution as "foreclosed," then she will need to move through an uncomfortable, faith-challenging experience in order to own her faith. Be encouraged—having students in transition is the goal.

Faith development in college is about owning your faith and practicing what you believe with integrity. Ultimately, we must act on our beliefs. Owning one's faith eventually means resting upon its precepts and acting accordingly. To be sure, we may not need to engage in every behavior in order to prove our faith, but at some point in the process our faith should direct our steps. An appropriate question that illustrates this ideal comes from the late Francis Schaeffer, a Christian thinker and writer, who asks a simple question: "How then shall we live?"

A residential community engaged in faith development is fluid and resembles a mosaic. An attractive characteristic of an educational community is that people are constantly changing; in fact, that is the goal. From one day to another students are moving from one "stage" to another. Just imagine what it looks like to have students on a floor moving from "foreclosure" into a "moratorium" or back the other way. Some students are coming out of a crisis of faith while the staff may be praying that others would enter into one. There is beauty in this mosaic of faith-developing students. If you gaze at the individuals that make up your living area, you can see that up close each person's experience is like intricate pieces of artwork. Yet when you stand back, you get a holistic perspective on what is happening in your community and see glimpses of how the intricate pieces work together. This larger picture is most often hidden from one's purview, but people of faith are given inklings of how each situation seems to have purpose. Scripture reminds us that God can and does use all things for his glory.

God is always at work. The great news for RAs—and all of us for that matter—is that we are not in this alone. For the person of faith, God is the one in control and we are but his hands and feet. What this means practically is that God can, will, and does use all aspects of each person's life to bring about change. We never know how or what God will use to influence change. It might be a kind word said in passing or the way a work-study supervisor handles a particular situation. The impetus for change may come from a faculty comment on a paper or how a difficult relationship concludes. The RA's role is like the farmer whose job is to till the soil, plant the seeds, weed, and water. It is God's role to bring about growth.

The "Now What": Practical Application of Faith Development Theory

Let's get really practical. The "now what" question is another way of asking Schaeffer's question; in light of all that we know "How then shall we live?" If an RA knows her calling and she understand how faith development generally works, this prompts us to ask the question, "What can one do to assist in the faith-development process?" Let's answer this question by looking at some general concepts of Christian faith development, and then we will revisit the eight dimensions of faith development provided by Benson and Eklin.

Start by listening to and following God. Remember, scripture reminds us that the human struggle is not as much with "flesh and blood" as it is a spiritual struggle. Trusting God to lead, challenge, and support one's efforts is where we begin. This means staying in scripture, praying, continuing to be a part of the fellowship as well as accountable to the larger residential-life staff community.

Stay connected to your staff and other leaders in the university. As we are seeing throughout this book, the whole institution is working on this issue. Partnering with other residence-life staff or other departments on campus maximizes your efforts.

The RA has many partners in facilitating faith development. You are not alone in this task. Your president, the administration, faculty, staff, coaches, and the facility service personnel are all working towards your institution's mission which includes a component of spiritual formation. The more one partners with other residential-life staff, the various campus-ministry personnel, and even the local community members, the better the RA programs will be and the more the RA can leverage powerful opportunities for change.

Be engaged and available. The ministry of presence is one of the most important and powerful tools. We see this in scripture beginning with God in the garden and we see it in the New Testament with Jesus becoming incarnate. Being present allows us to be known, to be trusted, and to be in a strategic position to act appropriately.

Look for the teachable moment. Educators understand that when you engage students in the learning process and encourage them to care about what they are learning, teachable moments emerge. Teachable moments can come at any time, so being available and intentional about facilitating faith development is vital.

God has made us communal beings. Humans are meant to thrive in community; even those who are introverted need others to challenge and support them. It is helpful to empower others within your residence hall to take on responsibilities that they can do better. Releasing others maximizes the strength of the community and can endear residents to one another. Good leaders empower others.

Speak the truth in love. We should not shy away from speaking the truth. But, as the RA challenges and supports those under her influence, it must be done in love. What this means practically is that the RA should understand those she works with and be careful to provide support with the challenge.

Illustrative Applications

To conclude this chapter, let's turn our attention back to Benson and Eklin's eight dimensions of faith development to see some practical, faith-developmental activities.

1. *Trusts in God's saving grace and believes firmly in the humanity and divinity of Jesus.* This first dimension is a starting point for faithful Christian believers—it is in this trust that everything changes. It is here in the salvation experience that one embraces an understanding of his or her need for a savior and accepts the indwelling of the Holy Spirit. The RA should, when appropriate, be ready to share her faith and provide direction for those wanting a personal relationship with Christ.

2. *Experiences a sense of personal well-being, security, and peace.* The RA has an opportunity to initiate focused programming, providing a scriptural perspective on human nature and how a biblical perspective impacts personal well-being and peace. These programs and follow-up conversations should be about who we are becoming when we are "in Christ." These programs and conversations may also focus on how students can live out this perspective. Partnering with the counseling center, the health-services personnel, or the chaplain's office are powerful opportunities to maximize the institution's resources.

3. *Integrates faith and life, seeing work, family, social relationships, and political choices as part of one's Christian life.* The RA's role in developing this dimension can take the form of programs and intentional conversations with students. Partnering with faculty members and individuals who are currently

in the workforce to dialogue about how they are attempting to do this can be a powerful opportunity for rich conversations. In addition, intentional yet informal conversations about the intersection of faith and studies or how athletes see their participation in sports as part of their religious life can be powerful exchanges. The career development center can assist in supplying these questions.

4. *Seeks spiritual growth through study, reflection, prayer, and discussion with others.* Here the RA can lead Bible studies, small groups, and prayer times, or partner with others on campus to assist the students in developing these spiritual disciplines. In addition, encouraging participation as a "living area" in campus-sponsored retreats maximizes the campus community's work. Conversations after these events can be rich and extend the learning. Utilizing partnerships with the campus ministries departments, the Bible department, and local church and para-church organizations may be of assistance.

5. *Seeks to be a part of a community of believers in which people give witness to their faith and support and nourish one another.* Connecting to others at an authentic level is one of the strengths of a community. This can be easier on a residential campus, but it must be nurtured. RAs must be intentional about developing a trusting, open atmosphere. In addition, most Christian colleges have a robust chapel program, and this can create a real challenge to get students to be a part of a local church community. We suggest that RAs should encourage their students to be a part of a local, multi-generational congregation.

6. *Holds life affirming values including commitment to racial and gender equality, affirmation of cultural and religious diversity, and a personal sense of responsibility for the welfare of others.* Our differences can either produce strife in our communities or create depth and richness. When leaders treat the "least of these" within our community with dignity and respect, this leads others to do the same. The RA's role is to model this dimension and also protect and support those within their community who are different. RAs can find help in many departments on campus, and in particular they may find additional

help from faculty, for example in the sociology and psychology department, or from the university's office of international and multicultural affairs.

7. *Advocates social and global change to bring about greater social justice &*

8. *Serves humanity, consistently and passionately, through acts of love and justice.* These last two dimensions are similar in that one's faith needs to be worked out in real life as the Apostle Paul suggested. There are many opportunities for an RA to partner with existing campus programs and to lead formal and informal conversations and programs. Having real conversations about the cause of poverty and a believer's responsibility to the poor and disenfranchised can be a real opportunity to explore and strengthen one's values and beliefs.

Conclusion

College is a spectacular time for students to rethink who they are and what they believe. College is also a time of significant change and transition. Exposure to new ideas helps broaden the student's perspective and strengthen ownership of beliefs. But, the process of evaluating, revising, and re-envisioning one's foundational belief system is hard work and for many students it creates crisis.

As the student leader who is living inside the community, your role in assisting students' faith development may be unparalleled. Knowing the faith-development process and facilitating developmental opportunities can assist your students in spiritual growth. Finally, acknowledging that the faith-developmental process includes struggle and crisis provides you a better understanding of what may be happening as students ask difficult questions and test their faith concepts. Remember, you are not alone in this work. God is constantly at work in ways you will never fully understand. We are blessed to be part of that work.

DISCUSSION QUESTIONS

Take a few moments and answer the questions. Jot down some of your thoughts under the questions for further discussion with the staff.

1. Why did you become an RA? What are your goals for developing the students in your area? Is there a connection between your goals and your institution's mission statement?

2. Identity development seems to be a central theme in psychology and faith-development theory. Do you agree that this is a primary outcome of the college years? Where do we get our identity and what does Scripture say about who we are? (Genesis 1; Psalms; Romans 3; and Ephesians 1 may help.)

3. Crisis seems to herald a significant opportunity for faith development. Jot down a few of the big questions you or your close friends have asked and how these questions impacted what you now believe.

4. Without using names, can you identity fellow students who are in the four different Identity-Development statuses described by Marcia? (Diffusion, Foreclosure, Moratorium, Achievement.) Do you agree with Marcia's statuses? Why or why not?

5. Questions, searching, and doubt seem to be a central aspect of the college years. What role do they play? How do you support those who are asking good questions without pushing them in the wrong direction?

6. Availability seems to be a central component of the work of a spiritual leader. How do you organize your schedule to maximize your influence (e.g., Are you a person who can be in a small Bible study group with your floor-mates)?

7. What are the formal connection points on campus for assisting you with helping your students mature in their faith (e.g. chaplain)? What are the formal connection points in your area that might assist in helping your students mature in faith (e.g. local Habitat for Humanity director)? Now think outside the box on who might be helpful in your work here (e.g. Skype with a Christian media personality that someone in your friend group has access to)?

8. What differing roles do God and you play in developing fellow students' faith? How do you assist God in his work? What part of their "success" is your responsibility?

Activities

1. Develop a spiritual formation program that has specific outcomes. Limit it to a one-hour program for the students in your area with a limited budget.

2. Develop a list of conversation-starter questions that you may wish to ask your friends or the students you serve. Think about how and when you might use these questions.

CHAPTER 6

The Role of the Resident Assistant in Working with Diversity

Listen, Love, Learn: Leading People Who Are Different Than You

Shirley Hoogstra and John Witte

Probably the hardest thing for me to adjust to when I became an RA was the fact that not everyone was like me. I mean, I know that sounds obvious, but before my RA year, I could choose my friends and who I spent my time with; and to be honest, that was easier. I chose people who I naturally connected with, probably because they were mostly similar to me. As an RA, I was challenged to broaden that out. Here was a floor full of residents, many of them very different from me in lots of ways. Some connected with me easily, and others kept their distance. I fought the tendency to play favorites with those who were more comfortable, and it certainly stretched me to open my eyes . . . and my heart.

No matter where you come from before your year as a resident assistant, you enter a new world, with new responsibilities and realities that will stretch you. To ensure that students can learn and thrive, you'll be asked to see the world (the campus) through a new set of lenses. Perhaps it's the lens of *safety and rule enforcement*, causing you to notice behaviors of others in ways you never had to before (e.g., asking someone to turn their music softer during quiet hours, or not to rappel down the side of their favorite campus building!). Perhaps it's the lens of *care and nurture*, where you'll strive to promote faith formation, or notice ways in which fellow residents might benefit from a campus resource (e.g., encouraging someone to talk with a counselor or chaplain, or to get a tutor for a difficult class). RAs most often, and appropriately, look through the lens of *community and commonality*, working to find ways to bring people together and to find unity as Christ followers. But another important lens for an RA is the lens of *difference and uniqueness*, where you pay attention to the unique and different ways God has created individuals in his image and given us life experiences that shape us differently. Noticing and paying attention to differences, as well as commonalities, is a foundational part of the RA role, and it can make you a better supporter, encourager, community builder, and friend. Our world, our communities, our churches, and our colleges need people who understand how to operate in an increasingly diverse world.

Now, you might already be asking why an RA would want to focus on differences when unity and community tend to be the buzzwords of campus life. In a nutshell, there are times when *not* noticing or acknowledging differences will do more harm than good, because differences are part of our stories. When you pay attention to differences between people in your living areas, you open yourself up to new observations and discoveries. These discoveries go beyond the surface-level differences you do notice, but which can easily be compartmentalized, minimized, or avoided. Is there someone on your floor from a different country or a different culture? You might notice that easily. But beyond the surface, how is that student uniquely wired because of her or his background? What makes her feel safe or valued? What is her communication style? What does she value about her faith that might be different or similar to what you value? What kind of school did he go to? Are his parents married or divorced, or has he lost a parent? Does the person have a different perspective on healthcare or taxes or the environment? These, and a myriad of deeper questions, apply to all of the residents of your floor—there is much below the surface. The answers to these questions are part of each person's unique story. It is to these stories that an RA needs to tend and be aware. We're always better at helping, guiding, challenging, and loving when we know another person's story. Doug Schaupp puts this in the context of Jesus' example:

> The practice of becoming captivated by people [springs] out of the life and heart of Jesus. Jesus could always see the unique beauty and the image of God in everyone he interacted with. He let all manner of image-bearing individuals interrupt his schedule and occupy his attention . . . . Jesus' life was marked by the kind of love that looks beneath the surface, and people flourished in his presence.

The lens of *difference and uniqueness* through which RAs view their residents is the same lens that Jesus uses to look at us. It is a lens that complements the unity and community that RAs strive for, because it helps us understand the things that might impede true unity and community. It adds vibrancy and richness. Living and working well with residents who are different than you provides an opportunity to see as Jesus sees and to help others flourish. We can't think of a better goal for an RA.

In the opening quote of this chapter, an RA reflects back on the experience and challenge of being an RA for people who were different. Go back and read the quote and try to guess the gender, or the ethnicity, or the disability, or the academic major, or the even the sexual orientation of the person writing that quote. The complexity of differences between people is real for *all* of us. The tendency to cling to the familiar or favor the comfortable is natural. To be an RA for *all* of your residents, no matter who you are or who your residents are, may take some work. Even students with more natural inclinations to seek out and accept differences between people will have blind spots.

Consider the diversity you will have in your living area to be an asset, bringing depth and meaning to a college education, as well as opportunities for growth and learning, particularly when differing beliefs and attitudes intertwine. As an RA, consider yourself the "conductor" who will direct the symphony of your living area during your year together. Sometimes the music will be pleasing to the ear and at other times it will sound like a first practice. But be encouraged—good, faithful efforts at engaging hard topics will be rewarding for you and your residents. You are a campus shaper in the way you model for others a willingness to promote community between people like you and those who are different. God made us all, and none by accident.

The Few in the Many

As we think about helping residents thrive and flourish, let's focus on students who may live in your area and find themselves in the minority—one of the few like them in a sea of people unlike them. While these could be any students, depending on the demographic of your institution, in the United States they have historically been students of color or international students at predominantly white institutions. Increasingly in our society and at Christian colleges, these could be students who identify as LGBT (lesbian, gay, bi-sexual, or transgender). Or they could be students with a particular disability. Think about the experience of someone who is *visibly* in the minority or someone who feels that way *internally* because the culture around them is predominantly different than theirs. They may feel that no one is like them or understands them, despite the well-intentioned outreach of a few.

> My RA was really friendly, but to be honest, I still felt really lonely. I know lots of us dealt with homesickness, but I was longing for more than my home. I missed friends who grew up like me, who understood my life, who didn't all come from same kind of church or high school. As one of the few African American students in my dorm, I sometimes felt like a visitor or an imposter. I felt like people watched me or kept their distance. I'd hear references to the "ghetto" or jokes about black names . . . all kinds of stuff that made it clear that some students had never imagined life in my shoes. Did they even see me?

Feelings of isolation can be compounded when a student feels she can't share an important or difficult part of who she is with others for fear of being excluded or judged.

> During the spring of my freshman year, I was eating lunch with
> a table full of friends and somehow the conversation turned to,
> "What if someone at our school is gay?" Most people were honest
> and said that gay people weirded them out. A couple of people
> said that they knew gay people and that fact didn't bother them.
> But one guy at the table said that if a gay guy hit on him, he would,
> "punch the guy in the face." Maybe he was trying to be funny, or
> the conversation was making him feel uncomfortable. . . . I can
> remember trying not to show shock, anger, fear, or anxiety. "Keep
> eating," I thought. "Don't look suspicious. Someone might notice
> that you're bisexual."

Perhaps you are a student who fits one of these characteristics or another, and you can relate to the experience of being in the minority. Perhaps you are a "majority" student who will be an RA for other students who find themselves in the minority. In all of these situations, there are some basic skills that you can bring to your year as an RA that will help you be the best RA for these students. These skills will sharpen your vision as you look at your residents with the lens of difference and uniqueness, helping them to flourish.

Recognize the Image of God

The first skill is to recognize the image of God in yourself and in all of your residents. Genesis 1:27 says, "So God created mankind in his own image, in the image of God he created them; male and female he created them."[2] Notice the individual and the collective nature of this verse. We tend to focus on the singular pronoun, which is certainly rich with meaning—each of us individually is made in God's image, in all our different gifts, interests, strengths, abilities, and creativity. The plural pronoun "them" is also rich—here we learn that the image of God includes humans *together*, male and female together. We hear an echo of this in the New Testament in the concept of the body of Christ,[3] where all the parts are important to the whole. Knowing that God can look at any of your residents and see a divine reflection, shouldn't we look at residents that way too? Knowing that God can look at your living community as the body of Christ calls us to do the same, recognizing the part that each resident plays. The image of God doesn't mean we're all the same, but it means we all have value and worth—in spite of, and because of, our differences. This is an important mindset to keep, especially when differences arise that cause division.

Beyond the concept of God's image, we share other important attributes that give us a foundation to be together. We share an identity as people created by God, broken and fallen in a variety of ways, saved by the grace of God shown through Jesus Christ, and able to participate in God's work here on earth. Like you, your residents chose a Christian college to attend and are making important decisions about majors and careers. Like you, they long to be known at a more-than-superficial level, emotionally and spiritually. They want to have friends, and college memories of late night talks, fun meals together, sporting events, Bible studies, and more. We're human beings, created by God to be in community with each other. When we can approach each other as children of God and fellow travelers on life's journey, broken but forgiven, we approach with the right heart perspective.

Grow in Self-knowledge and Knowledge of Others

The second skill needed in seeing your residents through the lens of difference and uniqueness is self-knowledge. Sometimes we go through life not thinking much about our own stories, about the things that make us unique, and about the experiences that have shaped our own attitudes and beliefs. We see differences in others using ourselves as the neutral middle. In talking about culture in a lecture to first-year students, Professor David Smith humorously remarked, "Culture is like bad breath—you recognize it in others but not yourself." We all have a cultural and ethnic background. We have biases and beliefs that come from family, friends, teachers, society, and the church, some good and some bad. If we've never interrogated our own backgrounds and assumptions, we might miss things to celebrate or ways in which we could be sharpened or corrected. We might miss ways that our actions or words inadvertently push people away or make us seem less hospitable, less safe. The first step to understanding others better is understanding your own story.

Out of necessity, students who find themselves in the minority have often thought about their own identity more deeply than others. When faced with feelings of isolation, lack of visible support, and even oppressive environments caused by the ignorance or intolerance of others, they are repeatedly reminded how their own culture or story is different than others. "Majority" students have the ability not to notice or think much about these differences—when you fit in, you tend to take things for granted. In the realm of cultural awareness, an example of this is the concept of "white privilege," which refers to the advantages in society that white people have because of their skin color, but to which they typically remain oblivious. Peggy McIntosh writes about white privilege in her essay, "Unpacking the Invisible Knapsack."[4] She says: "As a white person, I realized I had been taught about racism as something that puts others at a disadvantage, but had been taught not to see one of its corollary aspects, white privilege, which puts me at an advantage." Kristin Howerton put it this way in a blog post:

> Simply put, privilege refers to an unearned advantage. It usually refers to something inherent . . . something you were born with rather than something you worked for. . . . Racial privilege can take many forms, from minor things to life-threatening things. White privilege can look like being able to grab some shampoo at the grocery store and being confident they carry products for your hair type. White privilege can look like being able to find a band-aid that matches your skin tone. White privilege can look like walking through an upscale residential neighborhood without anyone wondering what you are doing there. White privilege can look like

wearing a baseball cap and baggy pants and no one assuming you are a criminal.[5]

Talking about white privilege sometimes aggravates white people, who might not agree or see advantages based on their skin color or who have faced disadvantages themselves. A full discussion of how identities and privileges (and oppressions) intersect is beyond the scope of this chapter. Every race and ethnicity has attributes of privilege and power—the strength and usefulness being dependent on context. But humbly wrestling with these types of issues is part of growing in self-knowledge.

Self-knowledge develops when we dare to share our stories with other people we trust, and allow them to ask us questions. We need to ask and honestly answer the tough questions about where our biases are, what stereotypes about others we believe, and what our families taught us about racial and cultural differences. We need to acknowledge what we don't know or understand, and then realize that learning about others and ourselves is a life-long process—a process that doesn't happen on its own, but rather happens when we are intentional about learning. We can do this in a variety of ways, including reading, attending lectures or training sessions, spending time with people different than us, and praying for the Holy Spirit to open our eyes.

Growing in self-knowledge goes hand-in-hand with growing in knowledge of others. Instead of seeing yourself as the neutral middle, you see yourself as one of many, able to compare and contrast your beliefs, attitudes, and experiences with those of others. You begin to see things you have in common as well as things that are different. Knowing about those who are different than you means respecting things that are important to them. One example of this is simply learning to use the language they prefer in referring to themselves. Is it "African American?" Or "Korean American?" Or "same-sex attracted?" Humbly asking and then respectfully using proper language for people is an act of hospitality. It communicates that you care and that you acknowledge an important part of who they are.

As you grow in knowledge of others, be cautious about generalizing that knowledge to all people in that group. For example, not all people with disabilities think the same about laws and policies. Not all Latino/a students are from Mexico or have the same opinions on immigration. Not every same-sex attracted male is interested in theater and not sports. We can fall into generalizations and stereotypes easily. Another caution is to avoid asking a student from an underrepresented group to speak on behalf of all people from that group. No white student is seriously asked what "all" white people think, and similarly no African American student could ever answer for all African Americans. When this happens, it simplifies and minimizes the complex stories we all bring to the table. And it can cause stress and discomfort for a student who is just trying to be himself or herself and not trying (or able) to represent an entire population.

Listening First

A third skill to learn and use when looking through the lens of difference and uniqueness is the ability to listen first. Beyond what you hear in a lecture or a training session or read in a book, try to learn from real people. This takes you beyond head knowledge into heart knowledge. And learning from real people means listening. Listening skills are usually high on the list of things that RAs learn during training, and they come in handy during all sorts of situations. Listening to someone who is different than you can be amazingly rich and also personally challenging. You might hear insights into a person's life that resonate with your own experience, or challenge your presuppositions about a person. You might laugh with the humor or cry with the pain. When you hear something you disagree with, such as a theological issue or a political viewpoint, you'll need to fight the urge to talk, to rebut, to disagree. Listening first means listening well, allowing the person's unique story to come out safely. Maybe conversations about disagreement will happen later, when trust is established—what's the rush?

> I remember going on a floor retreat and being given the chance to tell my life story, and feeling so nervous that others would just sit and listen. It was hard because my story isn't easy to tell. I think I went way over time, but no one cared. When I talk about growing up in my home country, there are things I don't wish to share. That night I opened up more than usual. When I was done, it was quiet . . . and then came the hugs.

Listening is an act of care and hospitality. The person sharing could be expressing a fear, or a joy, or a burden, or just a piece of who he is. Pray that God will open your ears to listen well, particularly when you recognize that someone is different than you. Hearing that person's story can be attitude changing.

> During my year as an RA, I had a resident share with me that he was gay. I never expected that to happen, and if you would have told me before, I think I would have been anxious about it . . . maybe even avoidant. But his honesty was amazing, and his struggle with stuff beyond what I had heard before really impacted me. What was probably best was that we talked about something really hard, but it wasn't hard. . . . He's a guy I know better now. Being gay is still something that is different between us, and not simple. But that's okay.

Creating a Safe Place for Living and Learning

A fourth skill to develop as you look at your residents through the lens of difference and uniqueness is the ability to be an ally, a friend, and a defender—so that all students can grow in faith and have a safe place to live and learn. Simply stated, an ally is someone who can *stand with you*, someone who speaks up on your behalf and protects you where you're vulnerable. Being an ally for a resident in your living area means being someone she sees as safe—safe to talk to, willing to share burdens, and trustworthy with confidential information. Allies create safe living areas by consistently addressing bullying or rude behavior toward others, standing up for those who are picked on, and even tending to the rules of life together in smaller things like noise violations or sports in the hallways. Allies don't blindly agree with or ignore all differences, but they ensure that everyone can feel the support of the community and a place to call home. The word "ally" can be politically charged in some circles. If you're uncomfortable with the word, don't use it. Instead, think of Jesus, who modeled coming alongside and standing with people who came to him.

When you stand with someone who is different, pay attention to language you hear that could be derogatory or insensitive. Jokes that come at the expense of other groups of people are not appropriate. Racial jokes or slurs are obviously off limits. The use of the phrase "that's so gay" as a put-down or of "homo" or "fag" creates an unsafe and uncomfortable environment for someone who is honestly working through issues of sexuality. When you pro-actively ask your residents to avoid this kind of language or confront it when you hear it, you are taking a risk that others will see you as overly sensitive. But you are helping to make a safe space where all students can thrive. Standing up takes courage, and standing alongside the vulnerable or oppressed is holy work. Christ's followers hear that call.

You act as a friend and defender for people who feel like outsiders when you go out of your way to make them insiders. When you plan an activity, think about whether everyone will be able to participate or whether the activity may feel exclusive.

> My floor had one resident who was in a wheelchair, and it was really awkward when we went on a retreat. All of a sudden we noticed how inaccessible the place was, and it was hard for her to get around the camp. I never would have noticed that before. Whenever we planned something after that, we just made sure to think it through and plan well, which wasn't really that hard. We just needed to do it. It brought our floor together.

Sometimes a difference in background will mean a resident avoids certain activities or traditions, which others can perceive as that student being judgmental, or snobby, or just not wanting to be involved. Thinking inclusively might mean ensuring a variety of activities and a low-pressure environment so that residents can choose to participate as time and interests allow. It means protecting the reputation of residents who don't participate in everything so that exclusion doesn't become the norm.

> A bunch of guys on my floor went paintballing one weekend. It turned into this big event with a sleepover at one guy's house, dinner with his family . . . and because I didn't go, I felt like I missed out. That is not my thing—we don't mess around with guns back home, and I had no interest, basically. Fortunately, that's not the only thing we've done as a floor.

Not Knowing It All

A fifth and final skill to develop as you look through the lens of difference and uniqueness is the skill of asking for help and giving yourself grace. You are not expected to be an expert in cultural differences, LGBT issues, intercultural communication, and so forth. But more than likely, you were hired to be an RA because you have the right heart perspective. You want to love your residents with the love of Christ, and you want to be part of the support and learning and development that happens in college. You recognize the richness of life together in community and you know that it doesn't always work perfectly. To do this job well, be teachable. Recognize what you know and don't know, and ask for help or training from the college staff. Use staff meetings and supervisory one-on-one meetings as places to ask questions, process your experiences, and learn. Your RA staff would be a great place to set goals and keep each other accountable to meet them. Sharing successes, as well as failures and mistakes, can be an important part of learning together and sharpening your own skills and efforts. Remember to remain humble; do not use a relationship with a student who is different than you as a badge of honor, to make yourself feel as if you've got it all figured out. Remember that the complexity of differences in people ensures that we'll always need to be learners and listeners.

Conclusion

All RAs will lead students in their areas who are different than themselves. It can be challenging to move toward those who are different, when our natural tendencies are to stick to the similar and familiar. But God has created all of us in his image, and he gives us the ability to learn from each other. He also calls us as leaders to look out for the vulnerable. As an RA, you will be called to look out for those who are different, particularly when that difference puts a person in the minority. There is much to learn about how to do this well, about how to view a person as more than just a cultural description or specific identity. Attributes of people overlap, and so do our beliefs, biases, and stereotypes. But if you commit to being faithful in your efforts, your experience of being an RA for *all* your residents will be much richer. Using the lens of difference and uniqueness will ultimately lead to a deeper sense of community as we allow God to teach us about others and tie us together in love.

In *Leadership on the Line* the authors give a powerful reason why people want to lead: "Leadership is driven by the desire of one person to contribute to the people with whom he or she [lives and works]. Love lies at the core of what makes life worth living."[6] We lead because we love people. Wanting the best learning environment for all students—those who are familiar to us and those who are different—is a way of loving people well. May God grant all of us the wisdom, compassion, and capacity to love as Jesus loved.

DISCUSSION QUESTIONS

Take a few moments and answer the questions. Jot down some of your thoughts under the questions for further discussion with the staff.

1. What role will diversity play in creating a "safe place for learning" on your floor this coming year?

2. What do I/we need to learn about myself/ourselves in regards to diversity issues on this campus?

3. What are the major diversity questions facing those on my floor?

ACTVITIES

1. Work with fellow resident assistants and role play conversations regarding differences you may face this coming year.

2. Spend time reflecting on your own thoughts/beliefs regarding the differences you may encounter on your floor. Discuss these with other RA's or your hall director.

CHAPTER 7

The Role of the Resident Assistant as a Peer Counselor

Knowing Your Limits and How Best To Help

Steve Morley and Sarah Hightower

The very existence of peer-leadership roles in higher education stems from the fact that we have great students. Think about it: we have students who willingly take on the responsibility of seeking the best interest of others. You are those very students. In the residence-life setting, what is so unique about your leadership position is that you are literally surrounded by your peers. You are willing to immerse yourself into a role in which you provide guidance and support around the clock and around the whole of the human experience; that willingness suggests to us that you and your fellow resident assistants have a deep sense of care and concern for your peers. This role of providing peer support has a high degree of transferability to other aspects of life. When this is done, the peer counseling role that an RA provides can be a source of growth, not only for the students you are serving, but also for you.

The What

Providing multi-faceted support to one's peers is central to the role of an RA. In my experience of working with RAs, and having interviewed nearly a thousand students interested in this role over the past fourteen years, it is common to hear that students' primary motivation for being interested in the RA role is care for their fellow students. While care takes many forms, RAs are uniquely positioned to serve as peer counselors to their fellow students. Let us examine a few major elements of this key support role.

First, while the term *peer* has already been used above, it is significant to note that you are a fellow student. Journeying beside your fellow classmates provides the setting for your role of peer counselor. The ability for you as a peer to relate to your fellow student based upon age, similar life experience—including common stressors and celebrations—serves as a vital aspect of the student care offered through the residence-life program. Further, as a peer, you can provide great assistance in translating policies, practices, and resources to other students. In fact, your position as a peer may allow you to be more effective in your service to your fellow students than professional staff simply because you can relate as a peer.[1]

Second, students who serve in this leadership role are likely the type of student who will naturally respond by caring and supporting their fellow students. As mentioned in the introduction, it is common to hear RA applicants discuss their primary interest in this role being that of care and concern for their fellow student. Therefore, it should be of no surprise that, when an opportunity to care and support a fellow student arises in the residence hall, the RA responds with a significant amount of invested ownership, not just as a RA, but as a caring student. The kind of students who express interest in serving as RAs are likely predisposed to give of themselves in settings that ask for the interests of another to be placed before their own. This characteristic is one which should be fostered, yet, to do so requires certain understandings: the extent of a student's ability to care for the needs of other students and the understanding of when a professional or team of students and professionals should be engaged in order to best serve all parties involved.

Third, students who serve in the RA role are uniquely positioned to care for others by their presence, which comes from living alongside their peers in a 24/7 immersive environment. The ability of the RA to serve as a positive example for others to follow is a significant demand given that the RAs live with those they lead. When this peer modeling is done well, it demonstrates a consistency of care that helps build the credibility of both the RA and the residence-life program as a whole. The consistent presence of the RAs in times of crisis, support, and celebration naturally leads to them being considered trusted sources of counsel.

Considering the unique role RAs play in the lives of fellow students, the kind of students drawn to this role and the setting in which they lead is critical to understanding healthy peer-counseling. The students drawn to this role likely care deeply for their peers and will probably seek to take on the challenges that their peers are facing as their own. While this is well-intentioned and a valuable characteristic, this tendency must be nurtured appropriately for the good of all students involved. Therefore, in an effort to develop this characteristic rather than merely consume this care for the good of the program, caution must be exercised in appropriately defining the role of the RA as a peer counselor.

The So What

In order to bring greater clarity to what is meant by *peer counselor*, we will offer contrasting examples in the hope that an appropriate definition of roles might result. In doing so, the merit of each role will be discussed while placing that role within a spectrum of student care.

First, it should be clearly stated: you are not alone. While your care for your fellow peer is to be commended, it is important to state up front that you are not alone in this endeavor. As such, you are not solely responsible for the total care of another person. This is not expected of you, nor are you adequately equipped to respond to every need of your peers. Your role is valuable, yet it is one role within a team of those who desire to care for and support you and your fellow students.

Counsel, not Counselor

Having said that, let's be clear: *you are not a counselor*, nor are you expected to be a counselor—at least in the sense of a clinical counseling relationship.

Rather, you are a trusted peer, a source of wise and caring counsel, an advocate for your fellow student who can listen, comfort, care, and assess, but who should not feel the responsibility to offer formal counseling. Your role is vital, yet you are not expected to know how to handle every situation that comes your way as an RA.

Let's consider what we can draw from this important distinction for a moment. A clinically-trained counselor is intentional enough to schedule their appointments in one-hour increments. They do so realizing the need for time and reflection in order for a conversation to be productive. Further, clinical counseling typically is not scheduled for late night or early-morning hours. The timing and setting of conversations on the wing versus counseling appointments simply suggest some basic, yet important difference between these two roles. Perhaps longer meetings are not better; perhaps meetings taking place in the wee hours of the morning are going to be somewhat limited in their effectiveness because of things like fatigue, concerns for the responsibilities of the next day, and stress. Finally, clinical counselors typically do not live right next door to those with whom they meet. Clinical counselors are typically not available with the same level of informality as you are as a RA, nor are they as socially, academically, and personally intermingled as you are. In some regard, the consistency with which you see your peers gives you an advantage over someone who only sees them in a one-hour setting. However, the concern here is that the kind of boundaries that are in place, for the good of all involved, are not nearly as easily established in a live-in RA role. Therefore, defining your role as a peer counselor should look significantly different than a clinical counselor. (We will further discuss how to establish healthy boundaries in your role as an RA later in this chapter.)

Challenge with Support versus Codependence

The idea of challenge and support is a concept that is central to the field of student development. Challenge is a viable means through which growth and development can occur, if an appropriate amount of support is provided. While challenge without support may lead to trauma, support without challenge can produce an equally undesirable result of codependence. As a peer, observing your fellow student encounter trials and hardships likely elicits a response of desiring to help. This is a good and admirable response. The idea of challenge and support suggests that the support that is provided must truly be in your peers' best interest. An appropriate level of support allows your fellow student to develop the necessary skills to address the current challenge. The way in which students are able to meet and resolve challenges impacts the way they view themselves, their surroundings (either positively or negatively), and their ability to meet and resolve future challenges.[2] Therefore, viewing challenge in this manner—as an opportunity for growth—serves to characterize it in a positive rather than negative manner.

Applying an *appropriate level of support* is key to understanding the way in which you as an RA can help your fellow peers. Challenges will come, and working in residence-life means that you will encounter a myriad of different life circumstances. Many of those circumstances are out of your control. What is within your control is your response and the type and amount of support you offer your peers. Positive growth can come from learning to navigate through challenging circumstances. In contrast, a diminished view of self and lack of ability can result from seeking to remove all challenge from a peer's life, thereby not allowing her to learn how to resolve those challenges on her own. While acknowledging the fact that challenges will come, I am advocating for equipping students to experience some degree of success in resolving those challenges. An appropriate level of support does not suggest one is completely dependent upon others for resolution, nor that the challenge should be removed entirely from their lives by those caring for them. Rather, one should resolve those challenges with the support of others.

Expertise and Experience

The familiarity you as a peer bring to the RA role is indeed a level of expertise. Your firsthand knowledge of the issues your fellow students are facing is certainly of significant value. Further, you are likely able to relate empathetically to your peers based on the similarities you share with them in age, experiences, and development. Something that I often share with my residence-hall directors is "No one can understand the life of a hall director like another hall director." The same can be true of many of the experiences of college students peers.

Your experiences as a fellow student can be drawn upon to teach those around you. Offering counsel based upon what you've experienced thus far in your life is an appropriate level of peer-to-peer counseling. You should feel equipped by those experiences to share with others, yet not feel responsible to have the answer to every question or circumstance that may arise.

The familiarity you share with your peers provides one important level of expertise. Another important perspective comes from the professional staff. Professional experience offers a perspective that has seen these (or similar) issues before and therefore has some awareness or means by which to bring resolution. This distinction is not meant to minimize the importance of the peer role in comparison to a professional. Rather, it is intended to underscore the need for both. Recognizing that there is indeed a difference in the roles that RAs and professional staff play in caring for students, it is helpful to consider: how do I know when I have reached the extent of my role and need to get others involved? Let us consider a few determining factors. First, remember how this section began: *you are not alone.* You are not expected to resolve all issues you encounter but rather to know when to involve others and who the appropriate "others" are. Second, as a peer, you should not feel the the burden of diagnosing the issue. Your observations combined with the insights of a professional staff member can lead to a well-informed and supportive response. Use your role to listen attentively to your peers. You will likely be approached with issues and questions that professional staff may not hear. Your life experience and training may equip you to respond with guidance that helps the student to resolve his or her issue. However, if you find yourself thinking "I don't know," be attentive to that as an indicator that you ought to involve someone else. So *listen*. Listen to your peer, and listen to yourself; when you reach the extent of your understanding, admit that and use it as a prompt to involve others in the situation.

Involving others exhibits consistency of care, for you are demonstrating a sincere desire for your peers to receive the full extent of the support they need to resolve their issues. Therefore, knowledge of the appropriate others to involve in the process of helping your peers will not only help your peers but also serve as a prompt for others who could perhaps continue the care for your peers beyond what you are able to do. For instance, knowing about the academic support service that provides tutoring and assistance to students struggling with a course equips you; you know that you do not need to be the expert in each subject area, nor do you need to provide the tutoring service directly. Instead, you may best help your peer by listening to his or her need, understanding your limitation as well as the expertise of others, and making a recommendation to involve others in helping with this concern. Other areas of support that should be considered are: the campus counseling service, campus police, career and vocational services, pastoral and spiritual life offices, financial aid, enrollment and retention offices, academic advising, dean of students, and dining services and campus nutritionist.

Finally, a word on involving others. As a trusted advisor and friend, you may likely hear from peers that they are considering harming themselves or perhaps others. In these situations, when someone's emotional or physical well-being is in jeopardy, involving the help of professional staff members is absolutely necessary. An RA may wrestle with how to do this and still preserve the peer's trust. I would suggest to you that, if your peer has trusted you enough to share this sort of vulnerable and personal information, he or she can also trust you to handle this information appropriately and involve only those who need to know.

Now What?

Having explained the unique role that the RA plays in providing peer counsel to fellow students and having made a case for understanding one's limits, we will seek to describe an RA's role as a peer counselor.

These pairs—counsel versus counselor, challenge with support versus codependence, and expertise and experience—are helpful contrasts and guiding principles as we define peer counsel and care. As we begin talking about *practicing* care, it is necessary that we are mindful that some of these practices will be natural to you and some will feel unnatural.

What does it look like to offer counsel?

For many, offering counsel is equivalent to speaking words of wisdom, encouragement, and challenge. While counsel definitely includes words, your presence and deep listening cannot be overlooked. These two practices—presence and deep listening—will help create fertile ground for words of counsel.

Presence

One of the names of God that perhaps is the most compelling for me is "God Immanuel" or "God with us." A central part of our Christian faith is the incarnation. It is no small thing that God himself came to us in human flesh.

Henri Nouwen, Donald P. McNeill, and Douglas A. Morrison remind us of the beauty of God's solidarity with us in life.

> God is a God-with-us, a God who came to share our lives in solidarity. It does not mean that God solves our problems, shows us the way out of our confusion, or offers answers for our many questions. God might do all of that, but the solidarity of God consists in the fact that God is willing to enter with us into our problems, confusions, and questions.[3]

My guess is that you can think of a time when you were lonely, hurt, frustrated, or afraid, and you can remember who sat *with* you in the hardship. While your words are incredibly important and can offer great comfort and counsel, you cannot discredit your presence. In this way, you have the beautiful opportunity and responsibility to be a representative of our incarnate Savior to your peers.

Nouwen, McNeill and Morrison continue:

> When someone says to us in the midst of a crisis, "I do not know what to say or what to do, but I want you to realize that I am with you, that I will not leave you alone," we have a friend through

whom we can find consolation and comfort. In a time so filled with methods and techniques designed to change people, to influence their behavior, and to make them do new things and think new thoughts, we have lost the simple but difficult gift of being present to each other. We have lost this gift because we have been led to believe that presence must be *useful*. [Emphasis mine][4]

I know that many of you deeply desire to be helpful to your peers, especially in times of hardship. But sometimes our desire to be useful gets in the way of our ability to care. You quickly find yourself ready to do something or say something and miss the opportunity to merely offer yourself—just your presence—to your peer.

Deep Listening

Listening can be an incredible act of care, an unexpected way to offer counsel. While we seem to fear listening or asking questions because we might not have the answers, we must remember that answers are not always what someone is looking for and that answers can be something others provide (perhaps a counselor, an RD, a professor, or a campus pastor). Even if answers are what the person-in-need wants, it seems that our human hearts universally desire to be listened to. To be known and heard. When you take the time to truly listen, you have the opportunity to provide space for someone to be known.

Kevin Miller identifies five helpful and practical tips for those who find themselves in positions of leadership and/or ministry. He suggests the following:

1. Listen without filtering
2. Discern without labeling
3. Invite without fixing
4. Follow up without nagging
5. Listen to the heart[5]

Let's briefly unpack each of these.

Listen without filtering. It takes work to truly just listen to someone, to turn off your mind and the distractions that come fluttering through it. Then, once you are engaged and truly listening to someone, you have to fight the temptation to make quick judgments, to make assumptions about what she or he is saying or not saying, and to refrain from coming up with the next question or your response while she or he is talking. Before you start a conversation with someone, take time to clear your mind of distractions. As you listen, instead of quickly summarizing her or his words, pay attention. Be curious about her or his choice of words. Pay attention to what she or he might be quickly dismissing. Sometimes we just need someone to listen to us. Sometimes through talking it out we find the counsel we need.

Discern without labeling. Few people like being known by an overly simplistic and often judgmental label. We, as listeners, can be quick to label because we want to fit people and their stories, issues, and problems into neat categories rather than understand and embrace their complexity. Fight the temptation to put a quick label on someone after hearing only a bit of her or his story. Instead, be curious. Ask further questions that get beyond the label and more into the core of who that person is, how she or he functions, what she or he is thinking, what she or he is feeling. Sadly, it seems to be especially easy to label each other when we talk about cultures, nationalities, sexuality, and struggles in life.

Invite without fixing. When someone comes to you with a problem or needs advice, a successful response would seem to be fixing his issue, situation, or problem. This does two things: it discourages growth in that person and does not empower him to grow in wisdom, and, perhaps more importantly, it puts you in a position to fix or save someone. The reality is that saving someone has never been the role of humans. Only the Holy Spirit can bring about change and growth. When focusing on fixing someone, you become narrowly concentrated on the problem (whether that be with the person or the situation in which he finds himself). Instead, invite others into the bigger picture of God's kingdom and help them discover where they find themselves within it.

This will both encourage and remind them of their identity and their place in God's story.

Follow up without nagging. It is not uncommon for RAs to have peers share a difficult situation with them and then for the RA to feel awkward or uncertain about how to continue the conversation. On the opposite end of the spectrum, some are continually reminding and hounding the person. Wherever you find yourself, following up after a conversation in which someone was vulnerable is vitally important. As you have put forth the good effort to be present and listen, following up completes the loop. Growth and change take time. Be patient, but also be intentional about furthering the conversation.

Listen to the heart. Without labeling and filtering, be sure to remember that there is a deep well behind someone's words. Students will feel cared for when they see you taking note of their body language, tears, excitement, fears, and exhaustion. Sometimes, words come easily to people and they can use them to hide the deeper sides of their lives, personalities, and experiences. Be wise and ask the Lord to help you see beyond the surface. Often, people have few words and will need your help to articulate what they are experiencing.

Practicing presence and deep listening will take significant work on your part as an RA. While it appears simple, you will need to put forth effort and discipline to offer care in this way. To the same degree, you will find yourself developing meaningful and transformational relationships with your peers that will afford you other ways to offer counsel.

What Does It Look Like To Offer Challenge with Support?

Sometimes you will not have the luxury of time. In most of the relationships you will build in your role, your presence and deep listening will provide fertile ground to challenge. While you will not have the expertise (nor should you), you cannot discredit your personal experiences and the significant amount of life that you live alongside your peers. Presence, deep listening, and challenge are all a part of offering counsel.

I would imagine that, as you read the word "challenge," many of you think "confrontation," "negative consequences," and "discipline." While these might be part of "challenge," that is not the description or picture we want to give you as you think about offering challenge in your role. Offering challenge is about inviting someone to be her best self, to be who God has called her to be. It means being honest but not condemning. It means speaking truth and sometimes difficult words, but not out of a posture of superiority or authority. Rather, it means encouraging and inviting others to participate in the ways God is working in their lives.

When challenge is framed as an invitation, it demonstrates great care. In contrast, denying someone those encouraging, inspiring, and life-giving words would be uncaring. The RA experience provides many opportunities to grow in our ability to care by challenge and invitation. Perhaps the difficult and most growing parts of the RA experience is that, as you challenge and invite those around you to be better, you will continue to live alongside them for the rest of the school year. While this is difficult, it is this longevity and consistency of relationship that will communicate care and support beyond the seemingly "difficult" conversations. This consistency of care after initial conversation is similar to the importance of following up after listening.

Sometimes our challenge is asked for, but other times we are called to challenge even when others might not want to hear it or are unwilling to receive it. In either circumstance, we must remember that people are complex. You could say something in the kindest, most uplifting and caring way, and it might still be received poorly. In these times, you must remember you do have a responsibility to offer counsel by way of challenge, and you are not responsible for how the receiver of the challenge responds.

Throughout most of your RA experience, you will likely learn about yourself along the way (often more than you ever imagined). Offering challenge is a growing experience for most RAs. Be gracious to yourself in this process, as well as humble with those you challenge. Allow yourself the grace to grow and change as the year goes on; enter into these situations of offering counsel—especially when it is one of challenge—with a humble heart and words.

Finally, remember that growth takes time. Just because someone is not receptive in an initial conversation does not mean that is how he will always feel or always think. We can all think of times when we have been challenged. No doubt, it was humbling, and, for worse rather than better, our natural response is often one of defense. However, that does not mean those words of challenge and invitation are not worth it. Remember the larger picture or the bigger perspective, and trust the Holy Spirit to work.

What Does It look Like To Have Appropriate Boundaries?

Offering counsel and offering challenge are impactful ways you can care for and serve your peers. We can, however, get weary of doing good. Most of you will be tempted to be a constant presence, always taking advantage of moments to speak into your peers' lives. You think, "How could they ever respect or listen to me if I am not there for their every need?" Perhaps this is a slight exaggeration, but the reality is that you desire to be in this position to help and serve. Also, it is easy, especially as Christians, to slip into the mentality that we can save everyone at all times. Wil Hernandez says, "The God-complex in us can readily take over if we fail to rein in our fleshly drive to act like the savior we are not. Only Jesus can fully come through for people."[6] This last section serves as more than words of caution but as crucial considerations to offering counsel. While it may seem counterintuitive, absence and solitude are necessary parts of peer counsel.

Absence

For many, absence from a person's life and from the hardship they are experiencing means neglect. Absence feels like you are ignoring someone's obvious need. However, absence is necessary for all of us in order to remember who God is. It is important so that an unhealthy dependence is not created between you and a student. Most importantly, when you withdraw from a situation or a person at appropriate times, this absence creates further room for the Holy

Spirit to work in his life *and* your own. Hernandez highlights the writings of Henri Nouwen on presence and absence:

> What Nouwen is specifically advocating is a more purposeful art of leaving—an act of "creative withdrawal." The rationale for such withdrawal is to pave the way for the Spirit of God to work freely in a person or situation without us potentially getting in the way. In short, "we have to learn to leave so that the Spirit can come."[7]

The beautiful reality is that your presence with people becomes all the more meaningful when you are also absent at times. Furthermore, your absence encourages your peers not to be dependent on you and empowers them in their relationship with God. It would be nice if there were a manual that said, "In circumstance A, be present for x amount of minutes and follow that with x amount of minutes absent." However, our lives are far too complex and complicated for a manual like that. Finding the balance between presence and absence will likely look different for each person and for each situation. Seek the counsel of your other student leaders and your RD as you grow in wisdom and discernment in "creatively" finding ways to both be present and absent.

Solitude

Finally, find times and places of solitude. Please realize that I am not talking about the half-hour you have by yourself as you get ready in the morning. Solitude is best done at length and with minimum distractions. Find long lengths of time (*at least* three hours) when you can put your phone aside, leave your schoolwork at your residence hall, and get away from campus. These mini retreats are needed in leadership and are vital to your capacity to care for others well.

Solitude allows us to be reminded of who we are and whose we are. Hernandez reminds us:

> The people whom we seek to accompany by our presence can detect, sooner or later, if we ourselves are disconnected from our

own soul and estranged from God, whose very presence we might not feel at all. As we equally grow at home with God and ourselves, others will feel increasingly at home with us."[8]

If the Son of God decided to take time for solitary communion with the Father, I think you can afford some time and space to do the same.

Solitude, similar to practicing the Sabbath, also helps us not think too much of ourselves and of the situations in which we find ourselves. At times, it may feel as though all you can think and talk about is a certain situation and how you need to be a part of it to help or offer counsel. In these times, we can lose sight of our humanness and often put less trust in God. We also lose sight of the larger picture and the promises of our Christian faith. The physical act of removing yourself from the location, people, and things attached to it allows the Lord to remind you of your capacity and how this seemingly overwhelming situation fits into his larger picture.

The role that you play as an RA in providing care to your peers is of vital importance to the residence-life program as well as the overall health of your college campus. While your role is distinct from that of the professional university staff, it serves to support the same overall goal of the growth and development of students. It is our hope that through a right understanding of your role, particularly when offering counsel to your fellow students, that you too will experience growth and development through serving as an RA.

DISCUSSION QUESTIONS

Take a few moments and answer the questions. Jot down some of your thoughts under the questions for further discussion with the staff.

1. If part of my role is to be present, when in the weekly life of my floor can I intentionally choose to be present? To just simply be?

2. How do I normally react when a peer or friend is experiencing hardship or difficulty? Am I comfortable with simply *being* with someone or do I feel antsy and unproductive? Why is that?

3. How might I live my life in a way that remembers the beautiful reality that God is with me and can offer his presence through me to others?

4. In my next conversation, can I be mindful of my tendencies? What am I thinking about when someone is talking? How quick am I to insert my own experience or advice? What is my body language saying? What assumptions do I quickly jump to?

5. What is my confidence level with offering challenge? What do I need to feel equipped to offer counsel? Spend time sharing these things with your RD.

ACTIVITIES

1. Describe to your fellow RAs a time that you felt challenged by someone else and how that person did it? Describe what you appreciated about that approach? Spend time asking your fellow RAs their stories of challenge.

2. Plan your weekly schedule for this school year and examine where there are gaps that you could plan for some solitude and time off campus. What will be important things for you to leave behind and take with you as you enter a time of solitude?

CHAPTER 8

The Role of the Resident Assistant as a Program Facilitator

Programming for Personal Formation

Stephen Ivester

After a Sunday evening discussion in a residence hall, I talked with a first-year student about what it means to be a man of God in college. He said, "This is the first community I've belonged to where I could be honest with other guys."[1] Being honest meant that he could bring his questions and doubts. He could share experiences and problems that sometimes kept him awake at night. Peers did not try to give him answers. Rather, they listened deeply. They honored him and his questions and were willing to walk into his questions with him. I believe that this candid community of men was one environment where his resident assistant deserved credit for thinking intentionally about how to facilitate growth in faith together through a consistent program on faithful Christian living. It was a time, twice a month, when residents were encouraged to bring all of their experiences, dreams, and questions to one another and then reflect together on how their Christian faith intersected with every area of their lives.

Many Christian colleges and universities claim that the best education does more than impart information and skills. At their best, these schools also strive for a holistic understanding of development. Indeed, this conviction includes a vision for personal formation. The Christian college where I work stands squarely in this tradition. Its catalog explicitly states that "our mission is not merely the transmission of information; it is the education of the whole person to build the church and benefit society worldwide for Christ and His Kingdom."[2] We also have a community covenant that explicitly lists these priorities. The covenant calls each member of the campus community to a lifestyle that involves "practicing those attitudes and actions the Bible portrays as virtuous and avoiding those the Bible portrays as vicious."[3] Among the virtues listed under the heading "Living the Christian Life" one finds the following: love, justice, kindness, compassion, self-control, forgiveness, chastity, and patience.

It seems clear to me that when we talk about the student living-environment at Christian colleges, the residence-life staff can have a significant impact if they connect their programming to the institution's mission. Creating space for their residents to be transformed and to become transformers is paramount. Therefore, resident assistants must develop a biblical vision for community wherein their programming is born out of a posture of personal and corporate formation into Christlikeness as Laurent Daloz maintains, transformative learning must always be integrally connected with social responsibility.[4] Certainly the student living environment calls students of faith to live out lives of compassion, righteousness, and justice and to strive to follow Jesus and invite each other to live into God's kingdom: ". . . to do justice, and to love kindness, and to walk humbly with your God."[5]

In this chapter, I discuss four conditions resident assistants can cultivate on their floors to enhance this growth toward personal and corporate formation. I then attend to practical program ideas that unearth tacit beliefs about college student identity development, lifestyle choices, and personal growth. Resident assistants must develop a vision for a holistic Christlike development of their peers as the foundation for serving and supporting their residents.

Creating Conditions for Programs

Daloz offers four conditions that can be cultivated in developing an ethos that fosters formation. The kind of environment Daloz invites us to create must include a place where (1) "the other" is present, (2) opportunity and processes lead to reflection, (3) role models and adults in the community engage each other, and (4) our learning leads us to act—that is, it becomes embodied learning.[6] What does this mean for the resident assistant?

First, resident assistants must push beyond complacent floor communities and foster an environment where everyone feels present. We live in a diverse world where homogenous groups of students can only lead to fear and hopelessness as we become less and less able to secure cultural uniformity. We need to encourage the development of inclusive, biblical communities on our floors where everyone experiences belonging. The emphasis behind this priority is expressed well by Phil Ryken: "The reason for this is not political, but biblical: insofar as possible, we seek to reflect the full diversity of the people of God as a visible expression of our unity in Christ and an effective means of preparation to advance the gospel worldwide."[7]

Advancing the gospel in our floor communities like this means we must understand that not everyone thinks alike and offer alternative ways of connecting in community. A resident assistant that I talked to recently has been learning to recognize unique differences in people and how to respond to and care for those students based on their background. Consider his scenario:

> I think it means as an RA I have to understand that dealing
> with people is done in different ways. Not everyone operates
> under the same rules or understanding of life. Our cultural
> heritage, socioeconomic background, personalities, and such are
> all so different. One student on my floor might come from an
> international background and need to be intentionally invited to
> an informal outing while another is totally comfortable with being
> spontaneous and on the fly. In these situations, I might have to be

more sensitive to some and say, "Hey, you're really welcome to join us here." And I might have to ask them twice.

Advancing the gospel in our floor communities like this also means we must seek to understand rather than refute. The college years are a great time to debate ideas and values, but we must learn to fight like we're right and yet listen like we're wrong. As we consider conversations like this, we let down our guard a little and practice what Mark Lewis calls an "immersion in liberal learning." He likens these conversations to "one[s] in which we deeply entertain the ideas of another—not because we will always agree with those ideas, but because in the process of considering them we become educated."[8]

If we are willing to foster this culture of inclusion in which everyone feels present and understood, we must learn to engage in deep listening. Listening well reflects a love for our neighbor, so we must love others even (especially) when we disagree with or don't understand their views. And we must be willing to change if and when we are persuaded that a different approach or view is more faithful. Speaking about a deep love for our neighbor, one colleague of mine noted:

> We must love our neighbors, especially our neighbors at the margins, those beyond the favorable light of power, outside the gate of privilege, beyond the pale of popularity, indeed, those that are distant [to us] and culturally different. Loving the neighbor requires this kind of active, sensitive, painstaking, time-consuming, self-giving appreciation and attentiveness to loving the other—and not others as I would like them to be or as I assume they are or as a means to my end or as raw matter for my project or as "the lost" that need to be led by me, but as real others in all of their integrity, complexity, agency, agony, beauty, and intrinsic value as people.

Resident assistants seek to develop this spirit of love among their residents and take every opportunity to cultivate this culture in their programming.

Second, the residential environment should be constructed so as to invite students into a process of reflection. This involves a safe space for the students to identify how far they've come along in their life journey and what challenges may lie ahead. This means that students take the time to suspend belief and to engage in "what if" thinking. It calls students to examine their own assumptions, and let go of them when they no longer serve them well. If not, they may end up keeping them, trapped in lose-lose situations. This in no way should communicate a total destruction of old understandings, but instead a remodeling to build whatever is true, whatever is honorable, whatever is just, whatever is pure, whatever is lovely, and whatever is commendable.[9]

If we are to create conditions that cultivate personal formation in this way, resident assistants will want to establish boundaries and structure to allow students to engage in the art of reflection. They must offer a vision for what might be and then encourage students toward a process of pursing formation through reflection. Creating this kind of environment for reflection requires resident assistants to be vulnerable with their floors. Honesty and integrity are fundamental. Resident assistants are not primarily answer givers. Rather, they offer resources, develop skills in reframing questions, offer new metaphors, and hold students accountable to their campus community's guiding covenants. Patience and sometimes silence will allow students to find their own paths to their own answers. Reflection is a journey, not just a moment, and it happens in community. This vision for reflection can be described in the following quote from a first-year student on my campus:

> I remember this event on my floor was really good because I
> had this "aha" moment and it just made me think about things
> differently in my life for weeks. So, I sat there and I felt stupid and
> like an idiot because all these upperclass girls knew so much of
> the issues and were so wise in thinking about the ethical dilemmas
> we faced and so forth, and these are things I never thought
> about before. To see these different values and ideas from these

relationships pretty much changed my attitude. It took a few weeks, but it was positive motivation for me.

Third, resident assistants are challenged to create conditions for formation where mentors are present and where students seek to learn from those who've gone ahead of them in their community. In addition to residence-life professional staff, many faculty, staff, administrators, alumni, local church leaders, and family members should be invited to be mentors, teachers, and role models in the residential environment. Well-selected adult role models can ask hard questions, listen, and often accept students where they are and for who they are. They sometimes cry with students, encourage students into healthy interdependence, and celebrate differences. Good role models engage students in developing a vision for their own lives and do not seek to make students fit their mold or coerce them to believe and act in prescribed ways.

Through these interactions with mentors, students can learn to see themselves through other people's lives. As adults share about what they are learning, the students likely will reflect on their own growth. Personal values become shaped by these relationships. In *Habits of the Heart: Individualism and Commitment in American Life,* Robert Bellah speaks about the importance of mentoring in community:

> We find ourselves not independently of other people and
> institutions but through them. We never get to the bottom of
> ourselves on our own. We discover who we are—and who we are
> meant to be—face to face and side by side with others in work, love
> and learning.[10]

The principle here is not only practical but biblical: Christ calls us to follow him in community, and in that community we find our true identity.

Finally, if resident assistants are going to create conditions for programming that fosters transformation, they must lead students to grow into and embody what they are learning on their floors. It is not transformative if it only involves their cognitive understanding. As the traditional Chinese axiom states, "Tell me and I'll forget. Show me and I may remember. Involve me and I'll know." Likewise, John Dewey said years ago, we learn by doing! Until learning is reflected in students' relationships with their peers, families, and other contexts where they live, worship, study, play, and work, they have not succeeded in what they set out to do.

Programming Ideas That Lead Toward Personal Formation

Now, wings formed and stretched in flight, we come to some practical programming ideas. It is my hope that these ideas will instruct and motivate you to a soaring adventure of learning together with your floor community. Here are five approaches to programs that you can incorporate in your floor community.

Faculty and Staff Conversations

Many college students are hesitant to initiate relationships with faculty and staff on their own. In order for students to feel more comfortable with faculty and staff, invite a range of women and men who can effectively engage with students to an after-hours meet-and-mingle. Take some time for these faculty and staff to share personal stories about internal struggles they faced in college, questions they had about God and faith, people that were influential to them, and how to prepare for a future job. This humanizes the faculty and makes them much less scary. And besides, most people enjoy talking about themselves and most students enjoy learning from others' experiences. Be intentional with these conversations and schedule a rotation of guests throughout a semester.

A Night of Questions

The college experience is generally a period where students dig up implicit beliefs about who they are, their major goals and aspirations, and their personal strengths and challenges.[11] Discovering what they believe about themselves occurs through the complex challenges of living and learning in a residential community. Inviting upperclassmen to a question-and-answer event in which residents ask tough questions about values, beliefs, struggles, and identity development can be a foundational crucible for students to glean habits and patterns that will help shape a vision for life beyond the college experience. Discussing issues of doubt, theology, individual competence, failure, and success all helps students conceptualize their own identities. This sort of life-on-life learning is essential for personal formation.

Institutional Climate

The unique institutional climate, history, and culture of each college and university may have an impact on how students are encouraged or inhibited in their growth. Exposing students to the legacy of the institution tells them the story they are joining. Incorporating both alumni and historic documents into a creative program can inspire students to embrace the unique culture of their campus. Additionally, since students are deeply impacted by the ethos of each institution, resident assistants should consider reviewing their institutional policies and procedures to examine where students find sticking points, ideological issues, or disagreements with lifestyle standards, then seek to build creative programming around those topics. It can be a powerful learning experience for students to research and debate both sides of an argument and wrestle with standards surrounding use of alcohol or sexual harassment. Engaging students in the objective, decision-making process of the institution helps clarify standards and brings deeper understanding and commitment.

Educationally Purposeful Events

Residence-life programming should not be seen as simply relational or social, but also a rich laboratory for expanding the cognitive growth and capacity of college students. Educationally purposeful events in the residence hall often shift the posture of how students learn; the informal nature of the learning brings about intrigue and motivation to learn. These events should focus on equipping students both experientially and in theory. Resident assistants should develop a few programs that directly connect with class topics like community development, global poverty, cross-cultural leadership, and intercultural communication as well as other hot topics like sexuality. Since college students have become increasingly interested in making their voices heard and are seeking to change the world for the better, it may be appropriate for resident assistants to work closely with expert faculty and student-affairs staff to develop these educationally purposeful events.

In general, these efforts would provide a breadth of knowledge, skills, modes of inquiry, and practices that might nurture Christian faith, encourage a pursuit of wisdom, and equip students for flexible leadership and service in the church and world. Generating discussion among students about important topics knits together the often-separate worlds of academics and student life.

Emphasizing a Theology of Christlike Engagement

Resident assistants should recognize the importance of being effective servants—on campus in particular and in life in general—with character, competence and confidence. They should affirm the values of leadership as selfless, relational, responsible, and visionary. Resident assistants can best serve students in their growth and capacity as servant leaders when they develop an intentional discourse that leads to a theological consideration of a theology of leadership that captures the example of Jesus Christ. His life and teachings illustrate foundational principles that are critical for college-student growth and development. It establishes for young college students a vision for a leadership identity in Christ. Leadership-development programs that establish this priority will effectively inspire the character, competence, and confidence necessary for developing the self-giving love for others that is essential for Christian students today.

Conclusion

Programming is an important element in achieving educational goals such as spiritual formation. Resident assistants need be intentional in providing programs that support and enhance the educational mission of their institution. In many regards, resident assistants are supportive educators in the development of their peers; therefore their programming should be built on a vision that complements the mission of the institution. There are learning opportunities throughout the entire college system and within every facet of the college experience. Resident assistants are not exempt from the opportunity to impact personal formation and should take this role seriously and be empowered and supported in these efforts.

DISCUSSION QUESTIONS

Take a few moments and answer the questions. Jot down some of your thoughts under the questions for further discussion with the staff.

1. Choose two of the most difficult people for you to relate to on a daily basis. If you were to reframe how you relate with them, what would you do?

2. Who is someone who listens to you with patience and interest? What are some principles of listening that you have observed in him or her that have been helpful to you?

3. How would you describe your commitment to reflection? What habits would you like to instill in your life to develop the skill of reflection?

4. What are the hot topics that need to be discussed on your campus that seem to linger without being actively addressed? In what ways might you develop a program that would enhance learning about one of those topics? What are some additional ways you might promote discussion about that topic?

5. Choose one of the programming ideas from the chapter: Faculty and staff conversations; a night of questions; institutional climate; educationally purposeful events; a theology of Christlike engagement. Identify one specific way you will implement your learning from this chapter.

CHAPTER 9

The Role of the Resident Assistant in Confrontation and Discipline

The 3,500 Pennies

Andre Broquard

The sidewalk from the dining hall at the institution I was working at went right past the front door of the residence hall where I was a resident director. One day as I was returning from lunch, an object came flying out of a third-floor window. I knew which room it came from—JD's, a large football player who had a bit of an attitude. We had crossed paths a few times already and now he was in clear violation of a residence-hall policy. Coincidentally, as I walked into the front door of the hall, JD's resident assistant happened to be in the lobby. I quickly told him what happened and told him to head upstairs to inform the residents that they would need to pay a fine for the incident. The fine would be $10 for a raised window screen and an additional $25 for the object that was thrown out the window. JD got upset and came down to see me. I gave very little opportunity for him to explain what happened and was not willing to reduce the fine. Shortly before the deadline to pay, JD arrived at my door with a large, heavy bucket filled with pennies and with a sarcastic smile said, "Here's my fine; you can count them if you want." I was frustrated, JD, was frustrated, and needless to say, this interaction did little to encourage our relationship and, in fact, created greater animosity. Not a great moment, but a good learning experience for me.

The purpose of this chapter will be to describe appropriate confrontation and discipline, to lay out an appropriate paradigm, to explain the RA's role in the process, and finally to offer helpful suggestions and guidance.

The What

Dreaded Confrontation (and Discipline)

It is rare for a student to apply to be an RA because they want to confront people and be a part of the discipline process. In fact, the resident director and director of residence-life might be somewhat hesitant to hire a student whose chief reason for applying was to confront people. Instead, most students pursue the resident-assistant position because of a positive, caring, supportive interaction they experienced with their resident assistants and a desire to share in the same way with others. In reality, being involved in confrontation and discipline may not even be on the radar of a student applying to be a resident assistant.

After resident assistants are hired and begin their training, most are nervous about their role in confrontation and discipline. During RA class and training, residence-life staff will spend time discussing ways to appropriately confront and describe their philosophy of discipline. Resident assistants will typically be given opportunities to practice and develop confrontation skills through role-playing activities and demonstrations. It is common for RAs to express apprehension when it comes their turn to engage a scenario. This is natural and expected. This chapter is written to reframe the confrontation and discipline process and provide a general "how-to" as you live with other students as a resident assistant.

Initial Thoughts and Perspective

It is a general human tendency to avoid conflict, and it does not change just because you are in a residence hall. As an RA, you will quickly see that students generally prefer to ignore an issue instead of addressing it. This happens especially in roommate relationships. An example of this is that students may confide in you regarding their frustrations with their roommate. When you ask whether they have shared these concerns with their roommate, you may get an incredulous, "No way! Why would I tell her?" This response may seem funny when you read it, but it is surprising how often it is said by friends, roommates, floor mates, and even parents. Research shows[1] that students go out of their way to avoid conflict. However, unresolved conflict is never healthy. As a RA, you will have the privilege of walking with students through difficult moments of conflict and, while you may feel the desire to avoid these difficult moments, embracing them can lead to powerful times of growth.

Furthermore, confrontation and discipline should be viewed as more of an art than an exact science. There are certainly solid biblical principles and relational skills that if followed help in confrontation; however, there are no clear cut, simple rules that apply to every situation. This is because human relationships are complex and messy. Every situation is different, and individual personalities bring their uniqueness into relationships. So, as you work with students, realize that it is too simple to identify a "right" and "wrong" way to confront. Instead, recognize that there many ways to confront and some work better than others. Next let's look at the reasons why we confront in the first place.

At the root of any confrontation and disciplinary action there should be the goal to honor and glorify God.[2] Let me encourage you to reframe confrontation and discipline as an opportunity to allow God's work to take place. It is not a negative interruption. This is a fundamental paradigm shift in perspective. This is especially clear in light of what was said above regarding students' desire to avoid conflict. So, when your goal is to honor God through your confrontation and discipline, there ceases to be an "us versus them" mentality. This removes barriers between you and the student. It communicates care, concern, and support, not judgment, condemnation, and resentment.

This leads to a second reason for confrontation and discipline. As RAs who are part of the residence-life department, you now are in a unique role of being both a student and a university staff member. You now represent the university and fill a role of connecting students to other university staff members and student development. In this role as student-staff, confrontation and discipline are important to upholding general, campus safety issues and university policies. For example, it is common for resident assistants to play a role in managing visitation policies. You may be asked to confront an individual who is unauthorized to be in particular location at a specific time. Most schools limit visiting hours for the opposite sex, so the RA may be responsible for "clearing" a residence hall of non-residents at a particular hour. Another example may be the need for a resident assistant to confront a student who has violated a university alcohol-use policy. In both of these examples, you need to remember your goal of glorifying God as you uphold and support a university policy or safety measure.

Confrontation vs. Discipline

For clarity, let me define confrontation and discipline. Confrontation is the initial acknowledgement that a violation of a policy has occurred. An analogy that I have used when I work with resident assistants is that confrontation is like turning on the light in a dark room. To explain, let me use a simple example from my family. My daughter really likes to play games on the iPad, but she must ask permission beforehand. From time to time I realize that she is curiously absent from our living room only to find her in her room with the door locked, sitting in the closet with the lights off quietly playing games. I have to unlock the door, open the closet, and turn the light on to find her. In a literal sense, the action of turning the closet light on allows both of us to see the situation more clearly. In a figurative sense, turning the light on brings attention to her behavior. This action of turning on the light allows us both to recognize that she is doing something that she should not do. In the same way, as an RA you will need to recognize the specific behavior in a caring, nonjudgmental manner by literally and figuratively "turning on the lights." This requires boldness, humility, willingness, and an observant set of eyes.

Discipline is the consequence or result of an individual's infraction of expectations. I believe it is helpful for RAs to think about these as separate actions. The discipline process involves some sort of conduct hearing to discuss the incident and future goals in order to provide appropriate sanctions or consequences.

Each institution follows its own clearly defined process for how to confront and discipline, but generally there is a time lapse between these two actions. Generally, the resident-assistant's main role is part of the confrontation while the resident director, director of residence-life, or maybe the dean of students carries out the disciplinary response. This separation of roles accomplishes three goals. First, protecting resident assistants from involvement in the disciplinary/conduct meeting keeps healthy boundaries in place for student-staff. Second, because of the more permanent nature of full-time professional staff, there is a greater chance for consistency, fairness, and reasonableness. Third, it provides fewer obstacles for the continued relationship between the resident assistant and the student after the situation. It is important for you to understand the unique expectations of your institution as you walk through these situations.

Assumptions in Confrontation and Discipline

There are three assumptions to remember as you walk with students through confrontation and discipline situations. First, the process is developmental in nature. That means the ultimate goal of the confrontation and discipline is to bring about growth. If our aim is to glorify God in conflict, then we will want to see the student grow into further Christlikeness. This development is stimulated when students live in a context of challenge and support.

Second, when possible, confrontation and discipline should take place within the context of relationship. This is really important and a major reason why the resident-assistant's connection with students is vital. As an RA, you should begin praying for residents before they even move into the residence halls. Once students begin moving in, it is imperative for you to begin building a sincere, authentic relationship with them. Jim Rayburn, the founder of YoungLife, a high-school evangelistic ministry, has been quoted as stating that you have to "earn the right to be heard." What he meant was that it is difficult to speak into and shape the life of another person until you have developed a relationship with that person. If you want to impact others and walk with them on their journey toward Christ, you must first show them that you care about them. You cannot rely on the fact that you are the RA. The power which comes with being a RA will not get you very far. You need to earn their respect and then you will have the opportunity to journey alongside them.

A third assumption is remembering to keep the end goal in mind. As you work with students "begin with the end in mind."[3] Being involved in other people's lives will be a messy process and take a lot of time. You need to remember that relationships take time, and seeing growth in a person's life will include hard and difficult moments. It will require you to make difficult decisions as you follow through on a policy when others want you to look the other way and pretend not to notice. Being an RA can be lonely during those tough moments. However, if you start with the assumptions that the journey toward Christ will contain deep valleys, mistakes, and bad decisions, then you will have the courage to walk the extra mile with them. We must recognize that we may not see their positive growth during a nine-month school year. However, we can trust that our sovereign God works with all.

So What

There are skills that, if you learn and develop them, will aid in confrontation and discipline. The first skill is difficult in practice—to listen to others. When I say listen, it is really more than hearing someone's words. Listening entails fully engaging the phrases, disposition, tone, and posture of the other person. This is especially important when you find yourself in a situation of confrontation. Listening requires you to refrain from speaking but also to use your ears, eyes, and whole body to discern what the person being confronted is really communicating.

This leads to a second skill. You will find that asking good, straightforward, value-neutral questions will greatly benefit your interaction. As you confront, you should "seek first to understand,"[4] and asking questions is a great way to get there. As you confront, remember your goal is simply to "turn on the light" in order to recognize an unacceptable behavior. You want to ask questions that establish the reality of what has happened.

The third skill may not seem like a skill, but is nonetheless an important aspect of confrontation. It is *time*. First, learn to invest time in people's lives before it becomes necessary to have a difficult conversation. Second, be timely in your confrontation. Discern carefully when to confront, but do not allow too much time to lapse. Third, as you are confronting a student, allow time to work. Or said another way, don't be afraid of silence and awkward moments. Allowing a long pause (maybe up to thirty seconds) after you ask a question gives time for the student to feel the weight of their behavior or decisions.

The Moment of Confrontation

As you find yourself in a situation needing to confront, you will enter that difficult, heart-racing moment. Let me offer some ideas for you to keep in mind. First, remember that your goal is to honor God and see God glorified in the other student's life. While you may be addressing a specific behavior, your hope is to see the student grow and help bring about holistic development. Addopting this attitude will reframe your conversations as well as your personal view of the student from one of frustration to one of support.

Second, don't assume you know exactly what is going on or what happened. If you make assumptions, you will normally end up being inaccurate about what really took place. So you must ask questions, even obvious ones. For example, JD's story at the beginning of the chapter illustrates the need for asking questions. Through observations, it was clear that something did exit the third floor window of JD's room. Beyond that, little else is known. As the RA entered JD's room, it might have been appropriate to ask, "Did something just fly out the window?" That is an obvious question. But the answer will give the RA entrance into further questions to discover the reason for the behavior.

At this point it is worth mentioning the role of emotions as we confront. Remember that emotions are good and God-given. Emotions bring richness and flavor to life. However, when unchecked, emotions can cloud judgment and lead us to do or say things we shouldn't. It is important to manage your emotions well and at the same time be very aware of emotions that are being displayed by the other person. You will want to avoid an emotional hijacking of your confrontation. This means that you must not let your emotions control your actions or words. This can be difficult, especially when other people are involved.

Here are two simple ways to manage emotions. One is by asking questions and seeking to understand. Another strategy is to slow the conversation down. Have you ever witnessed two (or more) people with uncontrolled emotions argue? One thing you might notice is that they speak, or more appropriately, yell, at each other in such a fast pace that there is no way to hear the other person. In fact, they really are not concerned about what the other person has to say; they just want to get their own point across. Little success can be found this way. But, if you slow the conversation down, emotions can still play a role without controlling the outcome. How do you slow the conversation down? Well, instead of responding to what the other person has just said, you can restate the point to make sure you understand them. Ask for clarification of the position, if needed. This strategy will break any rapid-fire exchange of emotional words or energy and instead allow you both to move toward recognizing the inappropriate behavior.

As you begin addressing the inappropriate actions with the student, you will eventually want to document everything you have observed. This step is important in recognizing and recalling what happened and will be very helpful as the discipline process continues. You will need to use all of your senses. What do you visually notice as your enter the situation or talk with the student? What do you smell? What do you hear and maybe even feel? (There may be a situation when your taste may help you observe what has happened, but I would not recommend your tasting anything). To be clear, using your senses to observe does not give free reign to open every drawer or the student's backpack. Furthermore, it would be a bit awkward and strange for you ask to smell the student's clothes. But you can use your senses to take in the general, plain-view surroundings of the immediate situation. For example, think back to the story at the beginning of the chapter. In this case, you may want to notice if the window is open or the screen is out, which would give you some indication of what happened. If the student responded with "no" when you asked if something flew out the window, you might be able to mention that the window is open and that you saw something come out of it.

While you are not a police investigator, being observant will help you, the RD, and the conduct officer with facts that will encourage truth and honesty. As a warning, it is helpful to recognize three common responses when people are confronted. They defend, deflect, and degrade. You are probably familiar with these and maybe even experienced them before. The defend response is when a student will attempt to justify his actions. The student may attempt to rationalize how his behavior is not wrong but actually positive. For example, a student may claim that their use of illegal drugs really helps them academically.

The deflect response is when the student deflects the confrontation by bringing up other students' behavior. She may argue about how what the other student did is worse, but she "got away with it." The deflection is an attempt to point at someone or something else. To keep the light from shining on her, they shine it on others.

The degrade response is a tough one. A degrading response is when the student points back at you and finds fault with you or blames you for what happened. The degradation is difficult to hear, but doesn't need a response beyond something like, "I am sorry you feel that way." It is important to remember that the degrading comments are spoken in haste and typically regretted, though this doesn't make them easier to take. However, choosing to extend grace to the student when he degrades you is a way to glorify God in the situation. All three tactics are used to move the focus off the actual situation. When defense, deflection, and degradation are used, it can be confusing because you are led into a never-ending philosophical discussion when all you really want to accomplish is to "turn the light on" the situation. The philosophical conversation is worthwhile and good, but don't get caught in this discussion when you are simply confronting a behavior.

After you have turned the light on by recognizing the inappropriate behavior, discovered what has happened, made sure the student is safe, and made observations, you will need to document the situation. Your institution will probably have a standard process for documenting these situations, so you will need to work with your RD to fully and accurately communicate the interaction with the student. Remember, documentation is vital in subsequent steps of the discipline process because you can give a first-person account. Your report sets the stage for the rest of the interaction with the student.

After you have conferred with your RD or supervisor and made the necessary documentation, an additional action is imperative if the ultimate goal is to be achieved. If the goal of conflict and confrontation is to glorify God and bring about growth in the student, then the relationship must continue. As the resident assistant, you need to reestablish connection with the student after the confrontation. This can and will be awkward. You may even get resistance from the student, but you need to sensitively pursue the student. The reason for the intentional pursuit is to reassure the student that the confrontation does not define or sever your relationship with him. Instead, as the resident assistant, you view the confrontation as a step into deeper relationship and an expression of commitment to the student's success and growth. So, you need to go back to the student and commit to a long-term relationship. Your re-initiation of contact will go a long way as evidence of your commitment to be a friend.

Now What?

The first part of this chapter defined and described confrontation and discipline. The stated goal of all confrontation and discipline was to bring glory to God and help others to grow into Christlikeness. The second part of the chapter offered practical skills that are helpful in confrontation. In this last section, I give five overarching words of encouragement in walking through conflict, confrontation, and discipline.

First, remember that you are not alone. While leadership is lonely and hard, there are people who want to support you. Your resident director will be a steady support and encouragement as you face difficult situations and messy moments. Your resident director has walked through situations before and has had many difficult conversations with students, so use him or her as a sounding board. The RD wants to help you be successful in your resident-assistant position and does not expect you to handle situations on your own. Be sure to talk with him or her before, during, and after confrontation moments. In addition, your fellow RAs are an additional resource. They can help you process conversations and situations. Of course you will need to be discreet with specific details and names in order to keep a situation private and protect a student's confidence. The other RAs on your campus are the only students who have some idea of what you are going through and may have had similar experiences. They are great people to lean on or give you space to decompress. Most importantly, the Holy Spirit is always with you. As believers in God through Jesus Christ, the Holy Spirit is with us in every situation and each conversation. Let's not forget the words of Jesus as he gives witness to the Holy Spirit in John 14:16: ". . . and I will ask the Father, and he will give you another Helper, to be with you forever." And then in Acts 1, just before Jesus ascends into heaven, he says, "but you will receive power, when the Holy Spirit has come upon you. . . ." It is great comfort to know the Holy Spirit is with us in every moment.

Second, difficult conversations and confrontation moments don't need to happen cold or unrehearsed. Wisdom suggests that you should think through your words beforehand and even practice what you plan to say with someone else. Taking a moment, maybe just stopping into your resident director's office or the room of another resident assistant on your staff, to share briefly the situation and what you plan to say will be helpful. It might prevent you from saying something that would hinder the student from growing. If time is available, you may even try writing out your thoughts. This practice has benefited me on numerous occasions, even when it was just minutes before meeting with a student.

Third, be yourself. It sounds simple but is a necessary reminder. You are not in this position by accident. While you are not perfect, you have been identified as having skills, abilities, and talents to be a resident assistant. Don't try to be more than who you are. Being authentic with students is likely to be reciprocated. If you have made honest efforts at building a relationship with a student from the first day and you approach any confrontation or discipline situation with the same relational attitude, you will avoid building walls or barriers. The relationship is the key, so pursue it at every turn.

Fourth, as you move through your time as a resident assistant, keep your heart and mind committed to glorifying God. In Colossians 3:17, Paul commends us with these words: "And whatever you do, whether in word or deed, do it all in the name of the Lord Jesus, giving thanks to God the Father through him."[5] Confrontation and discipline conversations are great times to apply this verse and commit to pursuing God and not our own desires or way. Even before you enter into the confrontation, take a quiet moment to pray this verse, inviting God to guide your words and thoughts during the conversation. We serve a loving, grace-giving, active God.

Finally, commit yourself to the developmental growth of others. By nature, growth that is developmental takes time because it is a journey. It is not accomplished with the waving of a magic wand. Real life is almost never made right in one day. Moreover, growth that is developmental will probably be messy and involve conflict. As a resident assistant, you are being called into this type of growth with other students. Confrontation and discipline are part of developmental growth by providing sacred opportunities to walk with others as Jesus did throughout the Gospels.

Conclusion

Having hard conversations with other students about their inappropriate behaviors will always be difficult and somewhat uncomfortable. It is helpful to simply acknowledge this reality, but it is also important to recognize the significant growth that often results from these conversations. Holding on to the fact that God will be glorified and the student will have an opportunity to develop provides incentive to enter into the hard situations.

Treat confrontation as a learning opportunity. You can learn each time you have one of these conversations. Remember, it is more art than science, which means there is no formula that you can apply to every situation in order to confront perfectly. Confrontation takes place within the context of relationship and can take many different directions. The key for resident assistants is to develop skills and abilities each time these types of conversations take place and apply the new skills in the subsequent conversations.

You have a choice in how you view conflict. The encouragement from this chapter is to change your perspective of conflict and confrontation to view it as an opportunity to glorify God. This change of perspective reframes confrontation in light of growth as opposed to hindrance. With this growth perspective, confrontation seeks to benefit the person being confronted by bringing about positive development. When you commit to the betterment of the other person, there is a fundamental change in the conversation. It becomes more of a side-by-side relationship instead of a head-to-head battle. Walking with another person to bring about Christlikeness is a wonderful opportunity and brings joy and fulfillment to the conversation.

Finally, confrontation and discipline allows you, as a resident assistant, to participate in the redemptive work of God. This is a worthy undertaking, and one that brings excitement and fulfillment. Trust God to do his work in and through you!

DISCUSISON QUESTIONS

Take a few moments and answer the questions. Jot down some of your thoughts under the questions for further discussion with the staff.

1. What was your reason for seeking the resident-assistant position? What percentage of it was for personal power, recognition, or growth of others?

2. What aspects of confrontation make you nervous or anxious?

3. What conversation skills do you need to work on to develop your confrontation abilities?

4. When you experience defend, deflect, and degrade tactics, which one will be most difficult for you? How might you prepare yourself to respond?

5. How will you use other resident assistants and your resident director for support as you confront other students?

ACTIVITIES

Think back to the most recent confrontation you have witnessed (maybe on TV, in a movie, or in real life).

A. Summarize the situation and then describe how the participants could have handled the situation better.

B. What aspects of correctly "handling the situation" would be easy or difficult for you, and how can you prepare yourself in those areas?

CHAPTER 10

The Role of the Resident Assistant in Self-Care

The Toughest Job You'll Ever Love

Kimberly Thornbury

In 1978, the Peace Corps launched a successful marketing campaign entitled "The Toughest Job You'll Ever Love." The advertisements caught the attention of those who wanted to sacrifice and serve to help others around the globe. While the resident-assistant job does not usually entail a trip to Africa, the position may be equally tough and is bound to stretch those who accept this challenge.

This chapter speaks frankly about RA self-care and how to prepare oneself for the journey of service ahead. Specifically, the chapter will deal with what an RA needs to know before applying for the position, four secrets to success once you have been accepted (including the five "golden phrases" of an RA), and four best practices that can help an RA thrive and avoid burnout.

Understanding the Role of the RA . . . Before You Apply

As freshmen, many of you may have been helped or inspired by an RA. Sarah was the nurturing RA who was there in the middle of the night when you were sick (without your mom) for the very first time. Mark was the cool junior RA who made you feel welcome without being overly smothering your first week. Paige was the genius RA who solved what seemed like your impossible freshman-roommate problem. How could you not want to be more like sweet Melody, whose event planning skills (and chocolate chip cookies) were near perfection?

Mature, wise, fun-loving, and caring—the RA serves as a role model. Like an Olympic figure skater who seems to twirl effortlessly on the ice, the RA can make balancing responsibilities seem easy to the outsider. But take a minute to peel back the layers, and the experienced RA may give you some advice before you dive into filling out your online RA application.

Even if you have lived with an RA, read the job description, and had multiple afternoon coffee talks with your resident director, the RA role is something you have to "experience." Even if you have spent an afternoon looking at resident assistant memes on Facebook, you will not completely understand the role until you have been in it. Written descriptions of the responsibilities are important, but you need to know that there are many aspects of the job that will be unexpected. For those of you who like to prepare and plan, remember that your personality needs to have some flexibility, because there are some aspects of the RA position that you can never anticipate.

The Model of "Exclusive RA Leadership"

Because of the breadth and depth of skills and time required, there is a growing model at many colleges and universities entitled "exclusive RA leadership." This means that if you are accepted as an RA, you may not be allowed to hold another leadership position, including university athletics. Stated differently, many colleges and universities understand that to be an effective RA, one cannot also continue serving as SGA president or on the student activities council executive team. While many students think they can "handle it all," smart universities understand that in the middle of the semester, while completing upper-level academic work, the RA role must not compete for attention from other organizations. Being an RA cannot be an "add on" to your existing busy-ness. While the residence-life staff will provide time guidelines, most RA positions demand twelve to twenty hours per week.

In short, being an RA requires commitment, which is why it is best to focus only on the RA position for the academic year. As a student, you do not want to become overwhelmed and resort to being "a canceller." While you often cannot cancel your responsibilities as an RA, you do not want to get into the situation where you have to cancel other activities midyear. Think ahead and do not take on too much. You can always add additional involvement later, but a good leader rarely says yes to something, only to say no later before the commitment is finished.

RAs are often top leaders, and have a servant spirit. Oftentimes the RA wants to be involved in multiple projects, and a person with an "RA personality" is usually asked to serve on several teams. A good rule of thumb is if the responsibility or involvement involves over a five-hour-a-week commitment, the RA (or potential RA) should ask the residence-life team for feedback. Often, any involvement over five hours a week needs to be officially approved by the residence-life professional staff.

On the other hand, residence-life staff are looking for RA candidates who have a connection with groups on campus. As the RA team works together to serve athletes, minority students, internationals, honors students, those involved in Greek life or SGA, they will be looking for candidates who have experience in and with those demographics. The resident-life team wants an RA team that reflects the diversity of the student body. Being an RA almost demands past outside involvement in specific groups, although while you are serving as an RA, you will have to limit your involvement in that organization (at least in a leadership role).

Being an RA is rewarding. You will have the ability to serve and shape others, and you will be working with fellow RAs and a residence-life staff who are committed to you. However, remember to count the cost before you apply. Saying yes to being an RA means saying no to other commitments.

Four Secrets to Success Once You Have Been Accepted

Congratulations! You have been accepted as an RA! Training will usually begin shortly after you receive the good news. According to a poll of seasoned RAs, five essentials can help you thrive as an RA, even before you officially begin. These essentials entail better-than-average time-management skills, having "the friendship talk," knowing and using "golden phrases," listing your life-giving activities, and understanding the best practices of a successful RA.

Time Management

The first five weeks of being an RA are a wake-up call. Even if you cultivated great time-management skills, and even if you knew August and September were going to be busy, you may struggle with the discrepancy between the hours in your day and your long to-do list. Most successful RAs not only *have* a calendar, but they actually *use* it! Determine a calendar system that works for you. Once you have identified the type of calendar, begin entering your classes, church or worship times, a regular sleep pattern (aim for seven hours each night), exercise, meal times, and study time.

Add to that list all of your RA commitments, including your one-on-one times with your RD, group meetings, working at the desk, and time for relationship building and event planning. Your family members would want me to remind you that they would love a time to talk regularly with you each week.

After all those responsibilities are filled in, show the schedule to a friend. Is there time left over? How much? Do you have any open time for emergencies? For friends? If you spend one hour a day on Pinterest or Facebook, did you account for that in your schedule? Be forthright and realistic about your time, write it down, and go over it with a friend. Trust me, this exercise will be both eye opening and instructive, and it must be done before school begins. If you want to lose weight, every calorie counts. If you want to save money, every penny counts. Thin people use their calories well. Wealthy people use their pennies well. People who manage their time well use their minutes well. Being intentional about how you will spend your time will reduce stress and burnout.

Entering activities into your calendar (scheduling alerts if you are prone to forget things) and taking time on Sunday night to review your week will help you feel more in control of your RA schedule.

Most people who are excellent time managers understand the power of habit and ritual. They get up at the same time, they roll out of bed and put on their running shoes without thinking about it, and they leave for class at the same time every day. They know which are their prime study hours and avoid distractions or other commitments during those times if at all possible. The more you can establish a routine for your day, the more effective you will be.

This is the principle of "muscle and mind memory." Establishing routines creates habits, and when habits are created, your body begins to do the activity without consciously deciding to do it. Stated differently, you do not waste much time deciding "what is next" because your body already "remembers" the next thing to do. This development of routines is particularly helpful for those who struggle with addictions to social media or have attention deficient disorder.

The Friendship Talk

Once you receive the good news about being accepted, no doubt your close friends will share in your excitement. They have talked with you about applying, encouraged you during the application process, and debriefed with you after your RA interview. These are the close friends who have seemed like sisters and brothers since freshman year. You value them, and you can't imagine the relationship changing.

As awkward as this sounds, before your RA responsibilities begin, you may need to have "the friendship talk" with these close friends. A new RA may need to explain to her good friends: "I may need you to pursue me more this year because my focus is going to be on my girls. I value our relationship, so I may need you to help initiate our times together. Our friendship is really important to me, and I don't want to get lost in my new responsibilities and neglect our time together." That may sound selfish, but managing expectations on the front end may avoid hurt feelings later. You can even "blame" the residence-life staff (or this book!) and tell them that you didn't want to have this conversation, but the book suggested that you do so. Alternatively, you could create "sacred times" to be with your friends each week. Without planning ahead, existing friendships can be crowded out by new responsibilities.

Five "Golden Phrases" an RA Must Learn

An effective RA must nurture and love others while also protecting his or her own time and schedule. These five "golden phrases" will not only transform the RA's time, but also make the RA more effective in his or her role.

First, "I care about this. Let's schedule a time to talk more."

Every student believes their issue is a critical emergency, and the RA is supposed to be responsive. However, most issues do not need to be taken care of right then and there. While living a life of "crisis and emergency" may make us feel important, it will quickly lead to burnout.

Listen to the "crisis" at hand, determine an initial solution, and then find a time that works to dig deeper into the issue. Remember, if you have planned your calendar well, you have time each day set aside to work on RA duties. This may sound cold and unresponsive, but if you give 100 percent of your immediate time and energy to every crisis, you may find yourself living in a world of crisis. In addition, a secret to success is *not* being available 24/7. You will gain more respect and may be more effective if someone needs to schedule time with you. Again, you need to balance handling the immediate crisis with scheduling time for effective follow-up. Trust me, the issue at 2 A.M. will still be there at 8 A.M. and most often can be dealt with at that time.

Don't be surprised if your resident director also is not available 24/7. He or she is placing these boundaries as a model for you. Many RDs will tell you, "Please don't contact me on Sundays or after 10:30 P.M., unless it's an emergency." The RD will usually clarify what is deemed an emergency (e.g. facilities emergency, student hospitalization, or unexpected moral issues that can't wait until morning.) If the RD can use this language with you, you have permission to use this language with the students in your care.

RDs are working full time, many have families, some are in graduate school, and all are juggling a full calendar serving in the student-services division of your university. In addition, many take Sabbath principles seriously and block out sacred time for solitude and reflection. As they model this for you, you should model this for your students.

Second, "Let me think about that."

The RA personality is usually a "yes" personality. Wired to serve if there is a need or request, the RA is usually in! Turning an automatic "Yes!" response into a "Let me think about that" provides you time (even if it's only thirty minutes) to calm down, think, and reflect on your existing calendar, goals, and to-do list in order to make a wise choice. Remember, you don't want to say yes to something now only to have to cancel later. Good leaders don't cancel; rather, they are smart about the things they say yes to on the front end.

Third, "Tell me more about that."

These are the five magic words in any relationship. Trust me, you can say these words five times in a conversation with someone, and they may not realize you keep repeating this phrase. Why? Because people want to be listened to and understood. This phrase communicates that you are interested in the other person and want to learn more. These five words can transform any relationship. Try it tonight on the phone with your sister, or with your roommate, or with that freshman in your hall who is struggling with homesickness. It allows the conversation to go deeper. The great RA uses this phrase in building solid relationships with others. When you build solid relationships, you can feel good about the job you are doing, and feeling effective at your job helps avoid stress and burnout.

Fourth, "Thank you."

A good RA models grace and kindness, and "thank you" is a key phrase that reflects these characteristics. A harried and stressed-out RA is not a good model for other students. Saying a sincere "thank you" after a compliment or after someone serves you, calms you down, and models excellence. Make use of this phrase a habit, and see how gratitude transforms other areas of your life.

Fifth, "I need help."

You have a color-coded agenda planner, but you never expected Anatomy and Physiology to be this hard. You never expected to be caring for a hall of freshman with so many issues, and you never expected your grandmother to break her hip right after fall break. Even the best time-management strategies cannot account for the unexpected events that bring us to the brink. Physical challenges and emotional relationship issues can be more than an RA can bear. Don't be afraid to ask for help. Your RD sincerely wants to know how you are doing, and to partner with you in putting together a plan to manage everything that is competing for your attention. Putting on a happy face when you need help can be dangerous. While you might not want to post a Facebook status about how stressed you are, it may be wise to plan a time with your RD (or school counselor or pastor) to talk honestly about how you are feeling. As an RA you are always giving to others, but there are many at the college who are invested in pouring into you as a leader. Let them.

Life-giving Activities

Before you begin your role as an RA, create a list of activities that you enjoy. Examples of these activities may include journaling, running, playing basketball, talking to dad, cooking, or listening to new music on Spotify. Are any of those activities in your daily, weekly, or monthly schedule? Before the crush of the semester begins, be sure you have that list written and posted in a visible place in your room to remind you what nurtures your soul. Without doing these things, you may become weary in your everyday tasks. Also, remember that not all life-giving activities offer the same refreshment. While you may love playing video games, too much playing can lead to depression and guilt. Activities that produce (knitting, cooking), reading good novels, exercise, and activities done in real time with others are more life-giving and refreshing than hours on social media.

One RA set a life-giving reminder alert via her phone to appear regularly. Every Friday afternoon the automatic message would pop up on her phone, "Have you cooked this week? Have you called mom?" She knew these two activities calmed her down and centered her, but in the midst of a crazy semester, she knew she had to make time for these life-giving activities. College is stressful and brings out vulnerabilities. Stress exacerbates these symptoms, but life-giving activities are one great way to combat stress.

Best Practices for Balancing Caring for Others and Self-care

Preparing in Advance for One-on-ones with Students Combats Stress

RAs care for others, both by planning activities that nurture community and walking through key decisions with fellow students one-on-one. To make the most of these one-on-one times, create small pockets of time before and after time with the student. Often an RA can be running from meeting to meeting, so creating these pockets of time can help reduce stress. Take a few minutes of time before the meeting and ask yourself three questions: "Who is coming?" "What is happening in his life?" "What do they need?" Focus on the student at hand during your time together, and schedule time to debrief after your meetings with the student. Leaders will tell you that the habit of a minute or two of reflection time before and after key meetings or activities is an important practice in successfully managing both activities and relationships.

Allow Your RD to Care for You.

As wonderful and kind as your roommates are, RAs need a "grown-up" nurturer. Your RD is usually asking, How can I love my RAs better? They are there for you. Your RD is there to listen to your troubles, because it is often not appropriate to work through your personal issues with the students you are trying to help. You need to be cared for so you are ready to greet whatever person or situation walks through your door. While you want to be "transparent" and "authentic" with the students under your care, it is a best practice not to use the students in your care to help you walk through your own personal issues and troubles. Again, you need to balance authenticity with professionalism, and an RA knows with whom to process personal problems.

The RD may ask if you have felt the freedom to shut your door this week. He or she may ask if you have felt the freedom to do your homework alone this week. Your RD is there to remind you that you are a student first. Your RD is there to help you grow as a child of God and to listen to how all aspects of your life are going. There is a saying that as long as you are counseling others, you should be in counseling too. Just as you will be helping and serving your students, so the RD's concern is to help and serve you.

Finally, in your individual sessions with your RD, talk about expectations. There is always more an RA can do, but you can get a more tangible sense of whether you are doing a good job by reviewing these expectations with your RD. It is a good feeling to know you are doing a good job and have a clear sense of your specific goals for the week. Talking about expectations can prevent burnout.

Solidarity with Other RAs

Be in regular prayer with other RAs. You will have a great fall/spring retreat, but after that group time you may feel scattered and isolated from other RAs. You may not actually see some fellow RAs for weeks, especially if they serve in another building. As you are praying for your fellow RAs, be encouraged that there is a group praying specifically for you.

In-service training sessions and fellowships with other RAs are often planned monthly. It is important to spend time with other people who understand what you are going through. Sharing a meal in the dining hall regularly is a great (and efficient) way to connect with others who understand the RA experience.

Select Good Roommates

This best practice cannot be underscored enough, as your room needs to feel like a sanctuary. Ideally, an RA should return to his or her room and not feel like they have to deal with roommate conflict. While many RAs secure a single room, some schools allow (or mandate) RAs to have roommates. Be sure to have a talk with your roommate about your role, including your time commitment, possible resident visitors, and the balance between being an RA and being a friend. Just because they are your roommates, they do not want to engage in any behavior that would place you in an awkward position, because although you are roommates and friends, you still serve as their RA.

Conclusion

Leadership requires you to be intentional about your self-care. Your time in the RA role will teach or reinforce principles about self-care that will go with you the rest of your life.

It is better to do a few things well then many things poorly, so choose your commitments wisely. The key phrases in an RA's repertoire (e.g. "tell me more about that") can be used in any position or role to build relationships and combat stress. Making time for life-giving activities will serve you well even as you balance your future job and family. Setting up boundaries and taking care of yourself in the RA role will not only help you thrive during the academic year, but will establish personal habits and patterns that will help you thrive through college and beyond.

DISCUSSION QUESTIONS

Take a few moments and answer the questions. Jot down some of your thoughts under the questions for further discussion with the staff.

1. Describe an RA whom you admire. In your opinion, what made that RA effective and/or influential?

2. What unexpected situations might an RA experience?

3. Which are you best at managing: Your money? Your calories? Your time?

4. Who is the best time manager you know? Why do you think they are effective?

5. Do you have daily habits now? Explain.

6. Which ones of the "golden phrases" will be easy for you to say? Which ones of these phrases will be difficult for you to use? Are there other phrases that may be critical for the successful RA?

Activities

1. Consider your current activities and involvement. What activities or organizations might you have to give up (or scale back on) in order to be an RA?

2. Make a list of activities that energize you. Note (realistically) how often can you engage in that activity this year.

3. Describe how you might or currently use a calendar or agenda book. Using a system of your choice, fill out next month's workload.

Endnotes and Bibliography

Chapter 1

Endnotes

[1] For a robust discussion of the founding and history of American higher education see Frederick Rudolph, *The American College and University*.

[2] Ibid.

[3] For a detailed description of the secularization process and the marks of institutions that have undergone secularization, see William Ringenberg, *The Christian College*, 113–82.

[4] Burton R. Clark, *The Higher Education System*.

[5] For a discussion of the necessity for seamless learning environments read "The Learning Imperative" distributed by the ACPA in (1996).

[6] Arthur F. Holmes, *The Idea of the Christian College*.

[7] American College Personnel Association, *Seamless Learning Imperative*.

Bibliography

American College Personnel Association, *Seamless Learning Imperative*, Washington, DC., 1996.

Clark, Burton R., *The Higher Education System: Academic Organization in Cross National Perspective*. Berkeley, CA: University of California Press, 1986.

Holmes, Arthur. *The Idea of a Christian College*. Grand Rapids, MI: Eerdmans, 1987.

Ringenberg, William. *The History of Protestant Higher Education*. Grand Rapids, MI: Baker Academic, 2006.

Rudolph, Arthur. *The American College and University: A History*. Athens, GA: University of Georgia Press, 1990.

Chapter 2

Endnotes

[1] "The Mission of John Brown University."

[2] Ibid.

[3] Ibid.

[4] Andy Crouch, *Culture Making*, 144.

[5] Ibid., 239.

[6] John Dewey, *Experience and Education*, 25.

[7] Ibid., 89.

[8] L. Dee Fink, *Creating Significant Learning Experiences.*

[9] www.CDC.cov/infectionsafety/pntalkit/section2spokesperson.html

[10] Timothy Keller, *The Freedom of Self-Forgetfulness: The Path to True Christian Joy*, 32.

Bibliography

Crouch, Andy. *Culture Making: Recovering Our Creative Calling.* Downer's Grove, IL: InterVarsity Press, 2008.

Dewey, John. *Experience and Education.* New York: Macmillan Publishing Co., 1938.

Fink, L. Dee. *Creating Significant Learning Experiences: An Integrated Approach to Designing College Courses.* San Francisco: Jossey-Bass, 2003.

Keller, Timothy. *The Freedom of Self-Forgetfulness: The Path to True Christian Joy.* Leyland, England: 10 Publishing, 2012.

Kraft, Richard and James Keilsmeier. *Experiential Learning in Schools and Higher Education.* Debuque, Iowa: Kendall/Hunt Publishing Co., 1995.

"The Mission of John Brown University," Accessed on July 21, 2015, http://www.jbu .edu/about/mission/.

Chapter 3

Endnotes

[1] Nancy Evans, Deanna Forney, Florence Guido, Lori Patton, and Kristen Renn, *Student Development in College: Theory, Research, and Practice*, 9.

[2] Ibid.

[3] Ibid.

[4] Ibid., 65

[5] Ibid.

[6] Ibid

[7] Ibid.

[8] Ibid.

[9] Ibid.

[10] Ibid.

[11] Ibid.

[12] Ibid.

[13] Ibid.

[14] Evans et. al,

[15] Ibid.

[16] Evans et. al,

[17] Ibid.

[18] Ibid.

[19] Ibid.

[20] Ibid.

[21] Ibid.

[22] Ibid.

[23] "What Will Your Verse Be?" Accessed on 7-27-15, https://www.youtube.com /watch?v=B2IaaFz4Fz4

[24] W. Whitman, M. Cowley, and E. Charles, E., *Feinberg Collection of Walt Whitman*

[25] Victor Frankl, *Man's Search for Meaning: An Introduction to Logotherapy*, 105.

Bibliography

Astin, Alexander W. *What Matters in College: Four Critical Years Revisited.* San Francisco: Jossey-Bass, 1993.

Chickering, Arthur W. *Education and Identity.* San Francisco: Jossey-Bass, 1969.

Erikson, Erick H. *Identity, Youth, and Crisis.* New York: W. W. Norton, 1968.

Evans, Nancy J., Forney, Deanna S., Guido-DiBrito, Florence., Patton, L. D., and Renn, K. A. *Student Development in College: Theory, Research, and Practice.* 2nd ed. Jossey-Bass Higher and Adult Education Series. San Francisco: Jossey-Bass Publishers, 2010.

Frankl, Victor E. *Man's Search for Meaning : An Introduction to Logotherapy.* 4th ed. Boston: Beacon Press, 1992.

Gilligan, Carol. *In a Different Voice: Psychological Theory and Women's Development.* Cambridge: Harvard University Press, 1982.

Parks, Sharon D. *Big Questions, Worthy Dreams: Mentoring Young Adults in their Search for Meaning, Purpose, and Faith.* San Francisco: Jossey-Bass, 2000.

"What Will Your Verse Be?" Accessed on July 27, 2015, https://www.youtube.com /watch?v=B2IaaFz4Fz4

Chapter 4

Endnotes

[1] Gen. 2 NIV

[2] Robert Zemeckis, *Cast Away*, (Hollywood, CA: Stephen Spielberg, 2001), DVD.

[3] Ernest L. Boyer, *Campus Life*, 179.

[4] Ibid.

[5] Ibid.

[6] Ibid.

[7] Ibid.

[8] Ibid.

[9] Ibid, 54.

[10] Ibid.

[11] M. Scott Peck, *The Different Drum*.

[12] Ibid.

[13] Ibid.

[14] American Association of Colleges and Universities, "Making Excellence Inclusive."

[15] American Council on Education.

[16] James 2:1–7, The Message

[17] Boyer, *Campus Life: In Search of Community*

[18] Eric Spiecker, "The Outward Bounds."

[19] Ibid.

[20] Ibid.

Bibliography

American Association of Colleges and Universities, "Making Excellence Inclusive." Accessed July 30, 2015, http://www.aacu.org/programs-partnerships/making-excellence-inclusive.

American Council on Education, Accessed September 2013, http://www.acenet.edu.

Boyer, Ernest L. *Campus Life: In Search of Community*. Princeton, NJ: Carnegie Foundation for the Advancement of Teaching, 1990.

Peck, M. Scott. *The Different Drum: Community Making and Peace*. New York: Touchstone, 1987.

Spiecker, Eric. "The Outward Bounds 'Temporary Community': A Practical Framework for Understanding Residence Life." *Acta Academica* 36, no. 3 (2004): 111–139.

Zemeckis, Robert. *Cast Away*. Hollywood, CA: Stephen Spielberg, 2001, DVD.

Chapter 5

Endnotes

[1] Matthew 28:19-20a

[2] Matthew 28:20b

[3] Arthur Chickering, *Educaiton and Identity.*

[4] James E. Marcia, Alan S. Waterman, David R. Matteson and Sally L. Archer, Ego Identity.

[5] Coalition of Christian Colleges and Universities. *Resource Guide for Christian Higher Education.*

[6] James E. Lowder, and James W. Fowler, "Conversations of Fowler's Stages of Faith," 133–148.

[7] Ibid.

[8] Fowler, James W., *Stages of Faith.*

[9] Peter Benson, Peter L. and Carolyn H. Eklin, *Effective Christian Education.*

Bibliography

Benson, Peter L. & Eklin, Carolyn H., *Effective Christian Education: A National Study of Protestant Congregations.* Minneapolis: Search Institute, 1990.

Coalition of Christian Colleges and Universities. 1998. *Resource Guide for Christian Higher Education.* Washington D.C.

Chickering, Arthur W. *Education and Identity.* San Francisco: Jossey-Bass, 1969.

Fowler, James W., *Stages of Faith.* San Francisco: Harper and Row, 1976.

Lowder, James E. & Fowler, James W. "Conversations of Fowler's Stages of Faith and Loder's the Transforming Moment." *Religions Education* 77, 2 (1982): 133–148.

Macia, James E., Walterman, Alan S., Matteson, David R. and Archer, Sally L., (1993). 2011 *Ego Identity: A Handbook for Psychosocial Research.* Reprint, Springer-Verlag NY.

Chapter 6

Endnotes

[1] Unless otherwise noted, all quotations are paraphrases of student stories, collected through anonymous assessment and reflection instruments over the years of our work at Calvin College. As such, they are representative of actual situations; though not direct quotes of identifiable individuals.

[2] Genesis 1:27

[3] 1 Corinthians 12:12–27 is a key passage for remembering we are image bearers of God who each have a role to play.

[4] Peggy McIntosh. "White Privilege: Unpacking the Invisible Knapsack."

[5] Kristen Howerton, White Privilege, and What We're Supposed to Do About It. Red Letter Christians

[6] Ronald A. Heiftz and Marty Linsky. *Leadership on the Line: Staying Alive through the Dangers of Leading.*

Bibliography

Heiftz, Ronald A. and Marty Linsky. *Leadership on the Line: Staying Alive through the Dangers of Leading.* Harvard Business Review Press, 2002.

Howerton, Kristen. "White Privilege, and What We're Supposed to Do About It. Accessed on January 27, 2014, http://www. redletterchristians.org/white -privilege-and-what-were-supposed-to-do-about-it.

Martin, Richard. "LGBT Feature: Richard's Story." *Chimes: The Official Student Newspaper of Calvin College.* Accessed July 30, 2014, http://www.calvin.edu /chimes/2013/11/14/lgbt-feature-richardsstory/.

McIntosh, Peggy. "White Privilege: Unpacking the Invisible Knapsack." *Peace and Freedom Magazine*, Women's International League for Peace and Freedom. (July/ August 1989): 10–12.

Schaupp, Doug. "Open the Parachute." In *Being White: Finding our Place in a Multiethnic World,* ed. Paula Harris and Doug Schaupp. InterVarsity,Press, 2004.

Chapter 7

Endnotes

[1] Steven Ender and Fred B. Newton, *Students Helping Students.*

[2] Nancy J. Evans, Deanna Forney, and Florence Guido-DiBrito, *Student Development in College.*

[3] Henri Nouwen, Donald McNeill, and Douglas Morrison, *Compassion: A Reflection on the Christian Life* (Doubleday, 1982), 12.

[4] Ibid, 11–12.

[5] Kevin A. Miller, "4 Conversations Skills That Transform."

[6] Wil Hernandez, "Henri Nouwen on Presence in Absence."

[7] Ibid, 20.

[8] Ibid, 19.

Bibliography

Ender, Steven C. Newton, Fred B. *Students Helping Students: A Guide for Peer Educators on College Campuses.* San Francisco, CA: Jossey-Bass, 2000.

Evans, Nancy J., Forney, Deanna. S. and Guido-DiBrito, Florence. (1998). *Student Development in College: Theory Research and Practice.* San Francisco, CA: Jossey-Bass Inc.

Hernandez, Wil. (2012). "Henri Nouwen on Presence in Absence." *Presence: An International Journal of Spiritual Direction* 18,3 (2012): 18–23.

Miller, Kevin A. "4 Conversations Skills that Transform." *Leadership Journal* (Summer 2012) Accessed on 7-29-15, http://www.christianitytoday.com/le/2012/summer/conversationsskills.html

Nouwen, Henri. J.M., Donald McNeill, & Douglas A. Morrison. *Compassion: A Reflection on the Christian Life.* New York: Doubleday, 1982.

Chapter 8

Endnotes

[1] Unless otherwise noted, all quotations are paraphrases of student stories, collected through anonymous assessment and conversations with students. As such, they are representative of actual situations, though not direct quotes of identifiable individuals. All conversations were conducted in confidentiality and the names of interviewees are withheld.

[2] "Wheaton Community Covenant," Accessed on July 27, 2015, http://www.wheaton.edu/about-wheaton/community-covenant

[3] Ibid.

[4] Laurent Daloz, Transformative learning in the common good, 181.

[5] Micah 6:8 ESV

[6] Laurent Daloz, Transformative Learning in the Common Good."

[7] Philip Ryken, "Student Life Diversity," Accessed July 27, 2015, http://www.wheaton.edu/Student-Life/Diversity

[8] Mark Lewis, "Theater as an Imperfect Mirror," in *Liberal Arts For The Christian Life,* Jeffrey Davis and Philip Ryken eds, (Wheaton: Crossway, 2011), 231.

[9] Philippians 4:7–8 ESV

[10] Robert Bellah, et al., *Habits of the Heart.*

[11] David Day, Michelle Harrison, and Stanley Halpin, S. *An Integrative Approach to Leader Development.*

Bibliography

Bellah, Robert, Madsen, Richard, Sullvian, Williams, and Swidler, Ann. *Habits of the Heart: Individualism and Commitment in American Life.* San Francisco: Perennial, 1985.

Daloz, Laurent. "Transformative Learning in the Common Good." In *Learning as transformation: Critical Perspectives on a Theory in Progress,* edited by Jack Mezirow, 103–123. San Francisco: Jossey-Bass, 2000.

Day, David, Harrison, Michelle, and Halpin, Stanley. *An Integrative Approach to Leader Development.* New York: Psychology Press, 2009.

Lewis, Mark. "Theater as an Imperfect Mirror." In *Liberal Arts for the Christian Life*, edited by Phillip Ryken, and Jeffrey Davis, 231. Wheaton: Crossway Publishing, 2011.

Ryken, P.: http://www.wheaton.edu/Student-Life/Diversity

Chapter 9

Endnotes

[1] David Day, Michelle Harrison, and Stanley Halpin, S. *An Integrative Approach to Leader Development.*

[2] Ken Sande, *The Peacemaker: A Biblical Guide to Resolving Personal Conflict* (Grand Rapids, MI: Baker Books, 1997).

[3] Stephen R. Covey, *Seven Habits of Highly Effective People.*

[4] Ibid., 235.

Bibliography

Covey, Stephen R. *Seven Habits of Highly Effective People: Powerful Lessons in Personal Change.* New York: Simon and Schuster, 1989.

Sande, Ken. *The Peacemaker: A Biblical Guide to Resolving Personal Conflict.* Grand Rapids, MI: Baker Books, 1997.

CPSIA information can be obtained
at www.ICGtesting.com
Printed in the USA
FSOW04n1736290915
11669FS